Simply Successful Appliqué

Foolproof Techniques for Hand & Machine

Jeanne Sullivan

C&T PUBLISHING

Text and Photography copyright © 2012 by Jeanne Sullivan

Photography and Artwork copyright © 2012 by C&T Publishing, Inc.

Publisher: Amy Marson

Creative Director: Gailen Runge

Art Director/Cover Designer: Kristy Zacharias

Editors: Lynn Koolish and Jill J. Mordick

Technical Editors: Helen Frost and Gailen Runge

Book Designer: April Mostek

Production Coordinator: Jessica Jenkins

Production Editor: Alice Mace Nakanishi

Illustrator: Jessica Jenkins

Flat Quilt Photography by Christina Carty-Francis and Diane Pedersen of C&T Publishing, Inc., unless otherwise noted; How-To Photography by Jeanne Sullivan, unless otherwise noted

Published by C&T Publishing, Inc., P.O. Box 1456, Lafayette, CA 94549

Library of Congress Cataloging-in-Publication Data

Sullivan, Jeanne, 1948-

Simply successful appliqué : foolproof techniques for hand & machine / Jeanne Sullivan.

p. cm.

ISBN 978-1-60705-480-1 (soft cover)

1. Appliqué. 2. Appliqué--Patterns. I. Title.

TT779.S853 2012

746.44'5--dc23

2012013361

Printed in China

10 9 8 7 6 5 4 3 2 1

Dedication

*To Dr. Eva Chalas, with skilled
hands and caring heart*

For saving my life

Thank you.

To my mother, resilient, patient, kind

For cloaking me in love and joie de vivre

I miss you.

In Grateful Acknowledgment

To my entire C&T team for working their incredible magic in the
preparation of the book! Brilliant!

To the amazing and generous appliqué quilters who gave so
willingly of their time and talents to make the Gallery possible—
every piece a confection. You inspire me. My sincere thanks to
Christine Bonney, Mary Cargill, Marlene Chaffey, Rosemary Clark,
Jean Clemens, Tina Cole, Ann D'Hondt, Janet Esch, Vera Hall,
Lynn Irwin, Tresa Jones, Nancy Kerns, Kelly Kout, Barbara Rausch,
Robbyn Robinson, Judy Shapiro, and Mara Warwick. "Goils, I couldna
done it withoutcha!"

To my friends and students who stood near, prodding me to begin and
then cheering me on to the finish line. Thank you for keeping me aloft.

To Patti Carey at Northcott for showering me with delicious
fabric in every color imaginable (and then some).

To William Sullivan, who took such wonderful
photographs when I ran short of hands, and
suffered the nightly glare of my OttLite
and laptop so that I could stitch and write
in bed. Thanks for all the home-cooked
dinners, Will!

To my family for their love, support, and good
times. Front and center, you enrich my life.

To God for daily talks, for helping me to stay
the course, and for the miracle of a new baby
grandson. I am blessed.

Thank you beyond words to each and all!

Appliqué

*Stitching little pieces,
Memories and dreams
Fingers busy sewing
A life within the seams.
Tiny scraps of fabric,
Bits of thread, I find
Time for quiet contemplation;
Peace and calm are mine.*
—Jeanne Sullivan

Contents

CD Contents

For bonus content for *Simply Successful Appliqué*,
see the following PDFs on the CD.

Introduction

Dear Reader,

Thank you for selecting Simply Successful Appliqué. I think you will agree that the most challenging part of traditional appliqué is to consistently and accurately turn the edges on appliqués so they have smooth curves, pointy points, and deep V's. For years I've been fine-tuning a method for helping students get over the turned-edge hurdles without becoming frustrated or giving up in exasperation. I was looking for a way to get them to the fun part of stitching quickly and without the difficulty of turn-as-you-go appliqué. I wanted a way that would ensure their success and confidence without compromising the beautiful, distinctive look of traditional appliqué. I wanted them to love appliqué as much as I do.

In this book you will see surprisingly easy, precise techniques for getting great results by hand or machine. Filled with success-oriented, visual step-by-step instructions, tips, how-tos, and projects, this book will provide you with skills and confidence so you can relax and enjoy creating beautiful appliqué right from the start.

I now find that the Simply Successful Appliqué techniques are so user-friendly, fast, and precise that I use them exclusively for my own appliqué, as do many of my students.

I wish you dancing needles!

♥ Jeanne

Tools

We live in a time of unprecedented choice when it comes to quilt-related supplies and materials. We surely would have been the envy of our great-great-grandmothers! But so many choices can be a bit overwhelming when it comes to selecting and deciding on just the right essentials. Where do you begin? How do you know which tools are must-haves and which are unnecessary gadgets?

The lists provided below are comprehensive. Not all the items are needed for every project. Most are readily available, and you may already have many on hand. The list is a starting place, with in-depth discussion relating to each item's specific use contained in the chapters that follow. These are the things that I have come to rely on and that work well for me for my Simply Successful Appliqué techniques. Please see Resources (page 126) for product availability.

Essential Tools

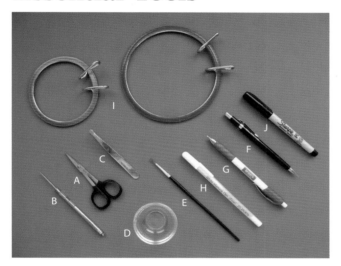

A Scissors: 4″, slim, with fine points

B Awl, also known as a stiletto

C Tweezers: with slanted, flat tips, not pointed

D Small glass bowl for liquid sizing

E Paintbrush: inexpensive, short handled (7″), pure bristle, round artist brush in a size #1 or size #2

F Mechanical pencil: 0.5mm lead size, Pentel

G Mechanical chalk pencil: 0.9mm chalk leads, Bohin

H White marking pen: Clover

I Embroidery hoops: 4″ and 5″ diameter, round

J Sharpie Ultra Fine Point permanent marker: black

Recommended Notions

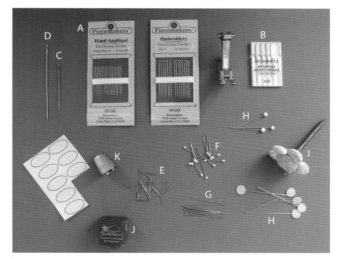

A Needles for hand appliqué: Piecemakers brand hand appliqué sharps, size 12

B Needles for machine appliqué: Microtex sharp needles size 60/8, or universal needles size 60/8

C Needles for hand embroidery: embroidery needle size 8 (for floss and #12 perle cotton); chenille needle size 22 (for #3 and #5 perle cotton); chenille needle size 20 (for #8 perle cotton)

D Needle for trapunto: doll-making (soft sculpture) needle

E Sequin pins: ½″

F Pearl-head appliqué pins: ¾″

G Silk pins: 1¼″

H Long quilter's pins: 1¾″ with pearl or flower head

I Pincushion

J Thread conditioner: Thread Heaven

K Finger protector: Thimble-It or metal thimble(s)

Supplies and Materials

A Thread for hand appliqué: YLI silk #100 or fine-weight cotton such as Mettler 60/2, Aurifil 50/2, or DMC machine embroidery thread

B Thread for machine appliqué: Mettler Silk Finish 100% cotton No. 50 thread for the bobbin, Sulky monofilament or Superior MonoPoly for the top thread

C Freezer paper: 8½″ × 11″ sheets

D Freezer paper on the roll: Reynolds

E Spray sizing (*preferred*): Magic Sizing Light Body; if this is unavailable, mix your own slurry from starch powder

F Clear, medium-weight vinyl: Quilter's Vinyl or upholstery vinyl

G Clear transparency sheets: Xerox brand; match type of transparency with printer type (laser or inkjet)

H Clear page protectors

I Cotton swabs and rubbing alcohol

J Water-soluble basting glue: Roxanne Glue-Baste-It

K Washable school gluestick: Elmer's

L Medium-weight interfacing: such as Shadow Block fusible lining from Jeanne Sullivan Design

M Nonwoven heavy interfacing: stiff enough, but softens with washing, such as Patch Back from Jeanne Sullivan Design

N Drafting tape

O Blue painter's tape

P Plastic storage bags: assorted sizes with top closure

Other Masking tape (*not shown*)

Equipment

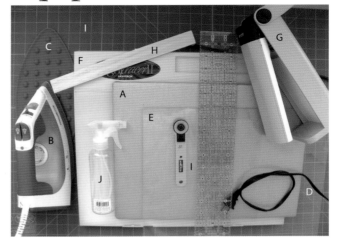

A Hard pressing board

B Iron

C Iron rest: for safety

D Extension cord (*if needed*)

E Lapboard: preferably clear acrylic plastic

F Lightbox: or lapboard with work light beneath

G Work light: bright, true-color daylight bulb

H Quilter's Tracing Bridge from Jeanne Sullivan Design

I Cutting mat, rulers, rotary cutter

J Spray bottle: with fine mist

Other Sewing machine with zigzag stitch: for machine appliqué (*not shown*)

Specialty Tools

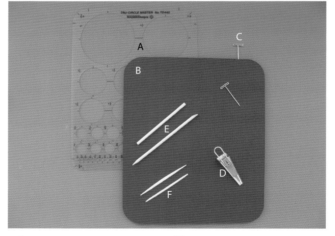

A Circle template master

B Mouse pad: ⅜″ thick

C T-pins: size 24 (1½″ long)

D Bias tape maker: Clover size 6 (¼″)

E Nail care / cuticle sticks

F Toothpicks

Preparation

Thomas Alva Edison said: "Genius is 1 percent inspiration and 99 percent perspiration." I say: "Appliqué is 1 percent inspiration and 99 percent preparation!"

This chapter covers the foundational nuts and bolts of appliqué. Learning about all aspects of preparation will help you to avoid pitfalls and frustration. Knowing the *whys, wherefores,* and *how-tos* will bolster your confidence, ensure your success, and have you enjoying each and every step of the process.

Color Planning

Color planning for a project is an integral part of the joy and magic of appliqué. Taking a drawn pattern and introducing fabrics in all their colorful, textural glory is nothing short of amazing! A few very fortunate and gifted people are natural-born colorists. The rest of us are mere mortals, who are stopped dead in our tracks when faced with choosing colors. Nothing else can more quickly turn our excitement about beginning a new project into uncertainty. Instead, let's turn these frustrations into fun.

Color Planning Inspiration

Nothing gets the creative juices flowing faster than an abundant selection of visuals. So, start collecting now! The sources for color inspiration are everywhere: mail-order catalogs from flower, fabric, and clothing companies; wrapping paper; decorator fabric; posters; designer silk scarves; magazine ads; greeting cards; wallpaper books; art shows; galleries; storefront displays; calendars; and more. The list is endless, and I haven't yet mentioned the Internet! Also, don't forget your camera. I take mine everywhere I go, and I'm continually delighted by the wellspring of color ideas I find in everyday and natural surroundings. Every time you have a pictorial source, pop it into a file folder. Before you know it, you'll have a rich personal resource just waiting to be tapped to get you started on your next appliqué project.

Color Planning Considerations

Color planning, fabric selection, and fabric auditioning are all related. Keep the following in the back of your mind as you begin to color plan an appliqué project:

- Select your background fabric color first (or near the beginning of your color planning). This is a good way to begin because you can then check that each fabric you add to the appliqué design will stand out against the background and won't get lost. Selecting a background fabric that is either dark or light in *value* will make it easy to find contrasting fabrics for your appliqué motifs. Whatever your decision, background fabric should not compete for attention with the appliqué design.

- Keep a design exciting and interesting with a mix of elements in your *color scheme* that include light, bright, dark, and dull. For most of us, our natural inclination is to stay in the middle-value range of color; it's our safety zone. Make a point of reaching outside your "same old, same."

- Consider the *scale,* which, as it relates to fabric, refers to the size of the design that appears on the cloth. Prints of varying scale will help keep your appliqué project visually interesting. For example, regardless of color, if you were to select all tiny prints for your project, it would read as plain and uninspired. Variety and contrast are characteristics to keep in mind.

Simply Successful Color Planning Approaches

Color planning can be approached in so many different ways—you're sure to find a favorite that works for you.

Color Planning Approach 1: Coloring

Remember how much fun it was when you were a child to sit down with a box of crayons and color pretty pictures? You'll rediscover coloring as a great way to approach a color plan for appliqué. Using photocopies of the master pattern will give you an opportunity to try out different ideas before you begin to pull fabrics into the equation. If you don't like something, begin again, using entirely different colors. It's only a piece of paper—there's no risk taking. Also, give watercolor pencils a try. They can be used dry (like regular colored pencils) but can also be dampened with a brush or cotton swab dipped in water for a blended watercolor effect.

Reducing the size of the master pattern allows you to fit four to six images on a sheet of copy paper. The smaller size makes it quicker to color and refine ideas.

Color Planning Approach 2: Fabric Toss

This approach is fancy free. Begin with the background fabric you want to use, tossing it down on the floor. Then, grab other fabrics and toss them on the background fabric. The color plan will take on a life of its own. It's a process of toss and take until you're happy with the combination. I like to stand so I can see the fabric choices grouped on the floor. This perspective gives me an accurate read on how fabrics relate and how the actual block will look.

Color plan developed with the fabric-toss approach. The results are the memory album (page 125).

If you'd like to give the fabric-toss method a try, refer to the master pattern to identify all the individual motifs, and then proceed to find fabrics for each.

Color Planning Approach 3: Selvage Dots

This method is so easy that I almost feel guilty when I use it. Whether using fabric from your stash or from a quilt shop, search for a multicolored printed fabric that appeals to you. Don't be biased by the subject matter. You don't need to use this fabric in your project—just use it to help guide your color choices. Refer to the dot lineup on the selvage to help you develop the palette for your project. Every single color will marry well with the whole. Guaranteed, you'll love the resulting color plan!

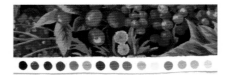

Select a printed multicolored fabric that draws you in. Then use the selvage dots to make your color plan.

One way to proceed is to select crayons or colored pencils similar to the dot colors and then color reduced-size copies of the master pattern (page 16). Another way is to make color photocopies of the actual fabric selvage that show the dots. Then cut apart the photocopied dots, using them as place markers: Move the dots around on the master pattern to identify your color choices for each motif. Enlist the help of tweezers to make it easier to move the paper dots. When you're satisfied with the color plan, glue the dots in place. Make a color photocopy of the plan or take a digital photo for reference.

Color Planning Approach 4: Fabric Collection

This is a fast and easy way to color plan. When fabric manufacturers introduce a new collection, the color palette has been developed so that all the fabrics will harmonize. By selecting fabrics from the same collection, you can be confident that your choices will coordinate well. Many times, a fabric collection will be offered in more than one colorway, just as you would find in wallpaper sample books.

The Internet is invaluable for exploring fabric collections. By searching for a specific fabric company, you'll find their current collections and be able to view the various colorways. Another good source is quilting magazines that feature designers, new collections, and projects made from the fabrics—a visual gold mine. Local quilt shops also like to highlight their new arrivals in collections before placing them on display in their color groupings. You won't go wrong buying several fabrics from the same collection to use as the common denominator for a color plan.

Sampling from Northcott's Heaven Can Wait collection by Ro Gregg, from which the fabrics for my Hope Sings design (page 124) were selected. With all the prints and colors harmonizing, I didn't need to concern myself with how the fabrics would relate.

Color Planning Approach 5: Clip Art

This approach can work wonders to unlock your creativity, and it has become one of my favorite ways to color plan a project. I call it *clip art* because it's very much like using existing image resources to build a collage, but with fabric instead.

When color planning *Springtime's Promise* (page 125), I began with a woven basket print that caught my eye. Then I chose the background fabric to offset the basket. I prepared the actual preturned fabric appliqués for the basket and placed them onto the background.

I proceeded to gather a lot of fabric prints, blenders, and textures from my stash. Then I began to clip small and partial flower motifs, a sampling of greens for leaves, and snippets of different fabrics that called out to me.

In this way, I could easily move the clipped scraps around until the plan for color placement pleased me.

You can eye the approximate placement of the snippets (leaves, flowers, and so on) or work with a lightbox layered with a copy of the master pattern and background fabric on top. The pattern lines will show through for you to clearly see where the appliqués or snippets should be located on the background.

Using my digital camera, I took this photo of my final clip-art color plan. I then printed a color copy to use as a visual reference when I constructed the appliqués.

Other Color Planning Approaches

For those who are computer savvy, the Internet offers untold treasures for color inspiration: from art, poster, and travel sites to flower photography and garden design. Other rich color-planning idea boosters can be found on scrapbooking sites and with scrapbooking software.

With Electric Quilt software programs you can color plan by importing your scanned appliqué design image and then auditioning actual fabric images. Use your own fabric scans or import fabric images from the Electric Quilt digital library (numbering in the thousands). When you come up with a workable version, it's easy to print a color copy to use for your visual reference.

Selecting Fabric

When choosing fabric to interpret your color plan, you'll find that the thrill is in the hunt. If you have a sizable stash, you can grab potential fabric candidates by the armful and try them out one by one. If you're just getting started, a trip to the local quilt shop with color plan in hand will give you a good start. Online searches are great as well, but understand that the color you see on screen is not always the *exact* color of the fabric.

Auditioning Fabric

No matter which method or process you use to come up with a color plan, you'll eventually get to the point where you've finished selecting your fabrics. You're satisfied with how they look as you squint your eyes, look up close, and preview from across the room. You've looked at it from every angle and every time of day and night. Yes, you're happy with the color plan! Well, don't be surprised when some of your choices don't quite work out. Sometimes fabric has a way of tricking the eye, and what looked great as a chunk of fabric doesn't translate well into an appliqué patch on a project background. By setting up a dress rehearsal, called *auditioning,* you can accurately appraise the merits of your fabric choices. Simply clip out snippets of the chosen fabrics and audition them on top of the master pattern. It is only when the fabric takes on shape and sits accurately next to neighboring design elements that we can more predictably determine how the actual appliqué will appear when completed.

While you're auditioning, you can easily adjust your fabric selection, color choices, or placement decisions and make changes *before* preparing and stitching the appliqués in place. It's far easier and much more fun to dance bits of fabric around on a piece of paper than it is to unstitch an unhappy appliqué from your background.

A colored copy of the pattern serves as a guide when auditioning fabrics.

Tweet Treats, color planned, designed, and stitched by author

Prewashing Fabric

The question of whether or not to prewash cotton fabric is often raised. My blanket answer is this: It all depends. If all the fabrics are cotton, just be sure to treat them all the same. If you prewash (a good idea for many reasons, but not always practical), then you should wash every fabric you plan to use in that project. Fabric finishes and residual dyes will also be removed during prewashing.

If you decide not to prewash, then that should be the rule for all. The reason is that if a quilt is washed and some of the fabrics shrink (because they were not prewashed) and some do not shrink (because they were prewashed), then you'll likely end up with all kinds of bulges and distortions.

Of course, if the quilt won't ever be washed, this won't be an issue.

Preparing Background Fabric

GATHER:
- Scissors
- Ruler
- Embroidery needle
- Background fabric
- Thread to match background fabric (with a slight contrast)
- Spray bottle with water
- Gridded cutting mat
- Hard pressing board
- Iron

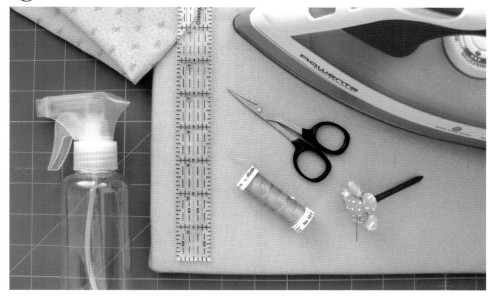

Determining the Size of the Background Fabric

The total size of the background fabric is determined by *adding* the size of the appliqué design, *plus* additional background to surround the appliqué (your personal choice), *plus* seam allowances, *plus* extra outside fabric allowed for shrinkage from stitching and trimming.

Example: The *Hope Sings* pattern has an appliqué design field of 11½″ × 11½″. Add 3″ for background around the design (allowing 1½″ for each side). Add seam allowances totaling ½″ (that's ¼″ on each side). Add 3″ more for fabric outside of the block (1½″ on each side). The total background fabric size is 18″ × 18″.

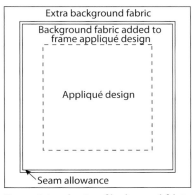

Extra background fabric

Background fabric added to frame appliqué design

Appliqué design

Seam allowance

Determining the size of background fabric

Tearing Background Fabric for a True Square

For appliqué (unlike pieced quilting), I recommend you *tear* your background fabric instead of cutting it. Tearing woven cotton fabric guarantees the fabric will be *on grain,* ensuring that your appliqué work will lie flat and the finished project will hang straight.

To begin preparing the background fabric, even up the crosswise grain: Tear it selvage to selvage. Next, measure, clip, and tear the fabric to the background size you need for your project.

Checking the Grain

Examine the *crosswise* (from selvage to selvage) edge of your fabric. The pictured edge has threads coming from it, called *checks*. If you pull a check thread and it leads deeper and deeper into the body of the woven fabric, the fabric was cut *off grain.* Tearing will true up the edge.

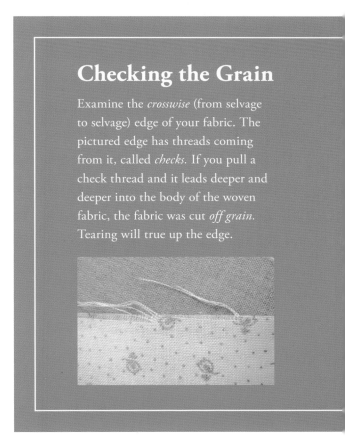

Stabilizing Fabric Edges

Tearing or cutting woven fabric interrupts the weave structure, causing threads to work their way loose from the edges. Stabilize the edges by removing about six threads from each side of the background, pulling them off gently, one by one. Alternatively, use a sewing machine zigzag stitch or serger to bind the edges, or use a bead of white glue or Fray Check to stabilize the edges.

Truing (Squaring) the Background Block

The goal is to prepare a background block that is a true square. The following instructions will ensure your background fabric is perfect for appliqué.

Place the block facedown on a pressing board. Bring up the bottom edge to meet the top edge, forming a rectangle. Check that all corners meet exactly, with the body of the fabric lying flat and the fold even. If all is well, your rectangle should look like the photo below, and you can then press a light crease on the fold with a hot, dry iron.

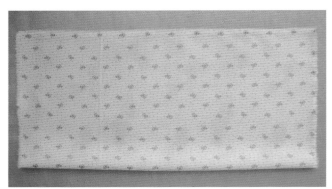

It's likely, however, that something will be askew, even if you prewashed the fabric. One of the top corners meets the top edge perfectly, while the other corner droops. If you try to adjust both top corners to meet, the fold is not flat and the body of the fabric is twisted.

If the block does not naturally fold into a rectangle with all corners meeting up perfectly (and most *will not*), then do the following:

1. Identify the drooping corner. In this example, it's on the left. **FIGURE A**

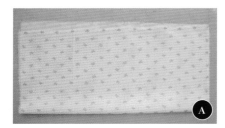

2. Pick up the drooping corner to make the block drape on its *bias*. Spray the entire block with a fine mist of water on the front and back. Wait a minute for the fibers to fully absorb the water. Pull on *opposite* corners to stretch the block along its bias. Don't muscle it too hard, but don't be wimpy either. After doing this a few times you'll get the hang of it. **FIGURE B**

3. Return the block, facedown, to the pressing board, bringing up the bottom edge to meet the top edge. Wetting the fabric relaxes it, making it malleable. Adjust and manipulate the fabric, coaxing the corners to meet and the body to lie flat with an even fold. Heat press *lightly* along the fold.

4. Open the fabric to expose the folded crease going down the middle. Orient the block facedown so that the fold is running vertically in front of you. Fold to match up both corners *and* the middle crease line. Manipulate the fabric until it is coaxed into alignment. Press the new fold with the iron. **FIGURE C**

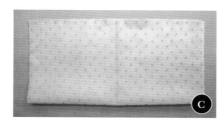

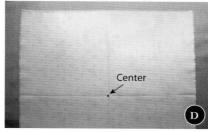

Center

5. Open the fabric. It is now squared-up along its crosswise and lengthwise straight of grain. There is no more skewing. Everything is true. The *center* of the background is where the fold lines intersect. **FIGURE D**

6. Double-check by lining up the folds with horizontal and vertical lines on a cutting mat. Slight adjustments, if needed, are quick to make. Just dampen and readjust the fabric. Remember, now's the time to address any discrepancy.

note *If you're planning to hand appliqué, the block is now ready to use. If you are machine appliquéing, a stiffer background fabric works best, so spray the front and back of the block with spray sizing, and heat set with a dry iron. Be sure to lift the iron and put it down as you press (instead of ironing back and forth) so that the block stays square.*

A Tailor's Tack to Mark True North

The background fabric needs to be oriented so the *lengthwise* grain (the direction of the selvage edge) is going vertically. This way the fabric will have the *least* amount of stretch when the block is placed in a quilt or hung on a wall. By tugging on both ends of the fold lines, you'll be able to identify the lengthwise direction—it is the fold with *no* stretch. To make it easy to identify as you work, make a tailor's tack stitch with needle and thread at the top of the fold. This will mark the top of the block, or true north.

Making a Tailor's Tack Stitch

1. Use a double thread about 14″ long; do not make a knot in the thread. Take a stitch with the needle. Pull the thread through, leaving a tail. **FIGURE E**

2. Repeat the stitch, using the same holes (right to left). **FIGURE F**

3. Pull the thread through. Cut the thread, leaving tails. **FIGURE G**

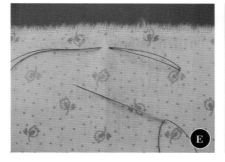

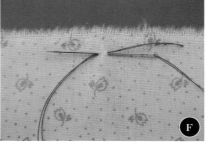

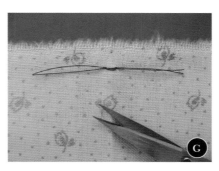

Adding Registration Marks

The creased folds on the background fabric point directionally *north, south, east,* and *west,* and will help to ensure the precise placement of the appliqué pieces. Humidity and handling will make the creased folds relax or disappear entirely over time, so marking the creases now while they are distinct will keep them accurate. Marks made at each fold are called *registration marks.* I prefer to make the registration marks with stitches. Washable markers will work, too.

Registration marks made with running stitches will remain on the block as a guide until the project is finished. It only takes a few minutes to stitch the registration marks, and you won't have to spend time testing chalk, pencil, or pen marks to see if they can be removed safely.

1. Use a double thread, knotting the end. With the block facing right side up, begin 2″ inside the fabric edge, taking small *running stitches* along the fold line toward the edge. Take a *backstitch,* ending with the needle and thread on *top* of the fabric. Cut off the remaining thread, leaving a ½″ tail. Repeat for the other folds. **FIGURE A**

2. Press the background flat with a hot steam iron. Remember to press rather than iron—you don't want to skew the background fabric. Do not be concerned if the folds don't completely press out. To remove fold lines remaining *after* the appliqué is complete, soak the fold line with a wet cotton swab; allow it to rest a few minutes (to saturate the fibers); then press with a hot, dry iron.

Appliqué Pattern Components

This section includes the getting-ready part of Simply Successful Appliqué. You'll learn how to make a basic appliqué flower, from start to finish, so that you'll understand the overall process and gain the technical know-how for doing any appliqué project you'd like to tackle. Just as important, you'll know the logic behind the steps.

Master Pattern

When we talk about a pattern in appliqué, it means the line drawing of the design. Just like in a jigsaw puzzle, individual pieces fit together to create the whole design. The pattern may be a simple motif, made up of only a few pieces, or it could be as elaborate as a Baltimore Album quilt block with 150 pieces or more. The appliqué process begins with a pattern design that is re-created with bits of fabric. An individual fabric piece is most often referred to as an *appliqué,* a *patch,* a *shape,* or simply a *piece.*

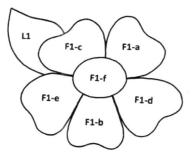

Master pattern for a simple flower. It is the F1 flower in the *Just for Pretty* sampler project (page 123).

I call a *labeled* appliqué pattern the *master pattern.* Labeling assigns a unique identity to each of the pieces. Labels aid in organization, especially if a pattern has a lot of pieces. All Simply Successful Appliqué patterns are labeled systematically. *Registration marks* are included on the master pattern. NOTE: These markings are critical for the accurate alignment of the appliqué pieces on the background fabric.

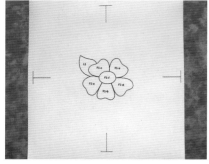

Registration marks on the master pattern

Preparing Working Patterns

Make three copies of the master pattern to be used (1) as a visual reference, (2) to audition the color plan (pages 10 and 11), and (3) to keep track of the prepared appliqués. All master patterns for the projects can be found on the CD, making it easy to print the paper copies you need. Depending on the pattern size, they can be printed on one sheet or multiple sheets that are then taped together for a full-size master pattern.

Preparing the Overlay

An *overlay* is a transparent copy of the master pattern that is placed on top of the background fabric. It is used to position the appliqué pieces in their proper place on the fabric. Following are two very effective methods for making an accurate overlay.

Method 1: Making a Clear Acetate Overlay

A clear transparency made with a printer or photocopier is the quickest and most *exact* way to prepare an overlay. Simply print or photocopy the master pattern onto a clear transparency sheet. Check that all registration marks have been copied. On the top edge, write *N* or *North* and draw an up arrow.

For a master pattern that is larger than the transparency sheets, photocopy the design in sections. Then combine the transparencies into the whole design, matching registration marks. Cut off any excess plastic and secure the seams with clear tape.

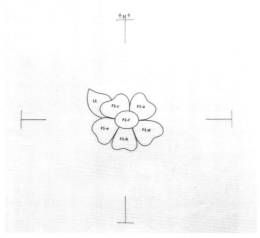

Transparency sheet overlay

Method 2: Making a Hand-Traced Vinyl Overlay

GATHER:
- Master pattern
- Clear vinyl, such as Quilter's Vinyl (by C&T Publishing)
- Sharpie Ultra Fine Point permanent black marker
- Drafting tape
- Copy paper
- Straightedge or ruler
- Cutting mat and rotary cutter (*or* scissors)

Vinyl offers a more flexible overlay material and is particularly convenient for large designs.

Trace the master pattern by hand onto a piece of clear vinyl plastic using a fine-point permanent marker. Vinyl is available by the yard in a variety of widths for creating overlays.

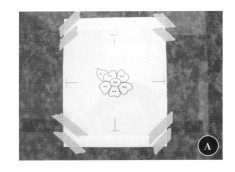

1. Work on a hard, flat surface. NOTE: A lapboard enables you to swivel and tilt the surface for comfortable hand positioning and more precise tracing. Begin by centering the master pattern on the lapboard, using drafting tape to secure it so it won't shift. Drafting tape will hold down the pattern securely but will not tear the paper when it is removed.

2. Cut a piece of vinyl large enough to include all registration marks plus ½″ extra on all sides. Center and tape the vinyl on top of the master pattern. **FIGURE A**

3. Trace the pattern onto the vinyl with a fine-point permanent marker. **FIGURE B**

4. Trace all the design lines. A quilter's tracing bridge (Resources, page 126) placed under your tracing arm (just past the wrist) will both raise and support your tracing hand while enabling you to have a longer, more controlled reach, resulting in smoother traced lines. Your hand will remain above the tracing surface, preventing you from smudging wet-ink areas. **FIGURE C**

5. Use a ruler edge to trace all registration marks onto the overlay. Make these lines *precise* because they need to line up with the sewn registration marks on the background fabric. **FIGURE D**

6. Check that all line work has been traced by removing the tape on the bottom edge of the vinyl and lifting it to compare the copy against the original.

tip *Inaccurate or stray Sharpie marks can easily be removed from the vinyl with a cotton swab dipped in rubbing alcohol. Dab any residual alcohol with a tissue immediately so it won't remove line work you want to keep!*

Rescuing Wrinkled Vinyl

Never use crumpled vinyl. It can be rescued.

1. On a pressing board, place cotton fabric underneath and on top of the wrinkled vinyl. Set the iron to a dry, very low setting—below synthetic. No steam! Iron, checking on the vinyl now and then by lifting the top cotton layer.

2. With patience, you can get the vinyl to soften and relax. You can actually remove every distortion and have a perfectly flat surface to trace on when you're done.

Template Patterns and Templates

How They Work

Template patterns are drawings of the individual pieces that make up the master pattern. They are used to make freezer paper *templates.* The freezer paper templates are then used to create the fabric appliqués.

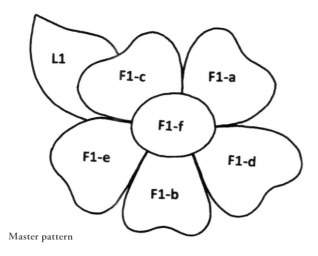

Master pattern

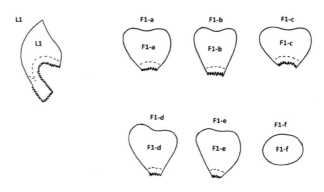

Template patterns made from master pattern

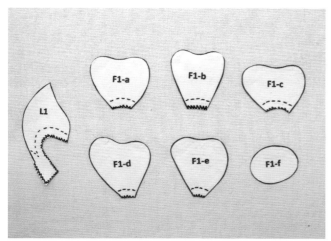

Freezer paper templates made from template patterns

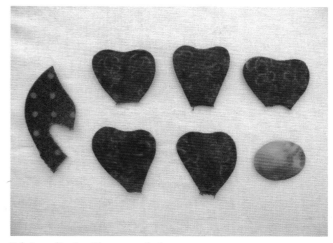

Fabric appliqués with preturned edges

Simply Successful Appliqué is a *prepared* appliqué method—the fabric edges of the appliqué patches are turned under and ready to stitch *before* they are placed on the background. Freezer paper templates make this possible.

 note *The fabric turn-under allowance in appliqué may also be called the* seam allowance, *the* turned edge, *or the* turned-under seam allowance: *similar names, same technique. All turned-under fabric edges are sewn to the background fabric with appliqué stitches.*

Appliqué Template Pattern Symbols

Solid lines represent the finished edge of the appliqué piece. This is the cutting line for freezer paper templates. Broken or dashed lines show where the next appliqué piece will overlap. Zigzag lines indicate raw edges that will be covered by the next appliqué piece.

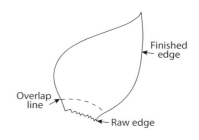

Template Labeling System

Labels for Template Patterns

Each template pattern has a label that includes an *uppercase letter* to indicate a design motif, such as L for leaf, F for flower, V for vase, and so forth. If a design includes more than one of a particular motif, as in three flowers, then each flower will be assigned a number (in ascending order): for example, F1, F2, F3. When a motif is made up of multiple pieces, the individual pieces are differentiated by *lowercase letters,* arranged alphabetically to indicate the order in which the appliqués will be stitched onto the background fabric. For example, if Flower 1 is made up of six parts, these will be labeled F1-a, F1-b, F1-c, F1-d, F1-e, and F1-f.

Labels for Optional Template Patterns

Very often the pattern directions will include *options* for how to interpret a design element in more than one way. For example, there may be an option to make a *one-piece* appliqué flower or a *multi-piece* version of the same flower. In this case, an additional set of template patterns is included. The template patterns are labeled using the same system but are *differentiated* with a star (★) preceding the template number; for example, ★F1-a. If a third option is given, then a third set of template patterns will be included, with a heart (♥) preceding the template number; for example, ♥F1-a.

Template Preparation

Just as there are many appliqué methods, there are myriad ways to construct and use templates. But, regardless of the method, the resulting templates must be *accurate.* It makes perfect sense: The closer the templates are to replicating the exact shapes, the more precise the finished appliqué project will be.

At the end of each project on the CD is a full-size labeled master pattern with a matching set of labeled individual template patterns. In this section you will learn how to use the template patterns to make the freezer paper templates.

GATHER:

- F1 flower master pattern (page CD29)
- F1 flower template patterns (page CD29)
- Freezer paper sheets or freezer paper on a roll
- Scissors
- Mechanical pencil (if using hand-tracing method)
- Hard pressing board
- Iron

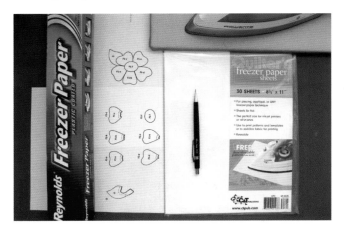

Making Freezer Paper Templates

Transfer Method 1: Printing Template Patterns onto Freezer Paper Sheets

The quickest and most precise method of getting the template patterns onto freezer paper is to print them directly from the CD onto freezer paper sheets, using an inkjet printer. NOTE: Do not use a laser printer. It can melt the freezer paper's plastic coating, with disastrous and costly consequences to you and your printer!

1. Load the paper feed tray with a small stack of plain copy paper.

2. Place a sheet at a time of freezer paper in the tray on top of the copy paper. Be sure to load the freezer paper so the print will appear on the paper (dull) side.

3. After you print the template patterns the first time, *before* making fabric appliqué pieces—

- Determine if the ink is heat resistant by running a hot iron over a small area on the *printed* side of the freezer paper. If the printer ink smudges, clean off the iron soleplate, wait longer for the ink to dry, and try the heat test again.

- Determine if the ink will remain set when it is wet by applying some sizing to the printed side of the freezer paper sheet. If the ink smudges or runs, fuse a second piece of freezer paper *on top* of the printed sheet. You'll still be able to see the markings through the second layer. Read about fusing freezer paper layers (page 21).

tips
Printing on Freezer Paper

- *Freezer paper is slick, and if more than one sheet is in the paper tray, it will feed into the copier unevenly. This can cause a paper jam and a ruined freezer paper sheet. Use only **one** sheet of freezer paper at a time in the paper feed tray.*

- *Freezer paper sheets tend to curl at the edges after they're removed from the packaging, and this may happen in only a few minutes. Curled edges interfere with the freezer paper feeding evenly into the copier. Carefully slit open the top edge of the plastic wrap and remove one sheet at a time, as needed.*

- *Avoid using a ballpoint pen or marker on the freezer paper; these marks can bleed onto the fabric when you're constructing the appliqués.*

Preshrinking Freezer Paper

Freezer Paper Fact 1: When freezer paper is ironed, it shrinks—not a lot, but it does shrink. If you're working with small pieces of freezer paper, the difference is minute. But in larger pieces or full sheets, shrinking can make a critical difference, especially with intricate appliqué designs and architectural details.

Freezer Paper Fact 2: Freezer paper, when ironed, shrinks more in one direction than it does in the other—the cross-wise grain shrinks more than the crosswise grain.

The remedy—preshrink freezer paper whenever you use it!

1. Place the printed freezer paper sheet (shiny side down) on a hard pressing board.

2. Set the iron to the lowest cotton/linen setting for dry ironing—no steam. Iron back and forth over the entire freezer paper area. It will adhere to the ironing surface. Small ripples or air bubbles may form on the paper surface. This is an indication that it is shrinking.

3. Peel off the freezer paper. Lay it back down and iron it again, leaving the paper on the pressing surface to cool a bit. The freezer paper should now be smooth. If not, repeat the process. When satisfied, peel off the freezer paper. NOTE: Do not preshrink freezer paper *before* using it in a copy machine. Print your copy first and *then* shrink it.

 tip *If the freezer paper is hard to remove from the pressing board, the iron is too hot.*

Fusing Freezer Paper Layers

For Simply Successful Appliqué, one layer of freezer paper is not sufficient for making a template. Fabric will be folded over the template edges when the appliqué pieces are made, so the templates need to remain rigid. Reinforce freezer paper templates by fusing them with a second layer of freezer paper.

1. Preshrink printed and blank freezer paper.

2. Cut apart the printed freezer paper template patterns into singles or workable groups.

3. Center the printed copy on top of the blank freezer paper (both shiny side down).

4. Fuse them together using a hot, dry iron and allow them to cool. Peel the freezer paper off the pressing surface. NOTE: If layers are not fused, iron longer or use a hotter iron setting.

Transfer Method 2: Hand Tracing Template Patterns onto Freezer Paper

Tracing by hand is an alternative method for transferring template patterns onto freezer paper. It's especially useful when working with enlarged appliqué designs with template patterns that exceed the size of a copier bed. Hand tracing also makes it easy to draw design changes, substitutions, or corrections. Work on a lapboard or other hard surface.

1. Cut a piece of freezer paper from the roll and preshrink. Use drafting tape to secure the freezer paper (shiny side down) on top of the printed template patterns. Trace around each shape, transferring all zigzags and dotted lines too. Copy all label information, both inside and outside of each template pattern. NOTE: If template patterns are not dark enough for you to see the tracing details, use a lightbox or tape the work to a window.

2. When tracing is complete, cut out around the perimeter of the template grouping and then cut and preshrink a second, larger piece of freezer paper.

3. Center the traced patterns on top of the blank freezer paper (both shiny side down). Fuse the 2 layers together with a hot, dry iron. Wait 15 seconds for the paper to cool. Peel the double-layer template patterns off the pressing board.

 tip *Allow fused freezer paper patterns time to cool. It's much easier to cut out and manage cool templates that will lie flat.*

Appliqué Basics

This chapter focuses on Simply Successful Appliqué basics: making and basting fabric patches prior to stitching them onto the background. The F1 flower in the *Just for Pretty* sampler project (page 123) will continue as a working example. Whether you're planning to appliqué by hand or machine, all Simply Successful Appliqué preparations are the same until it's time to stitch the patches onto the background fabric.

For inspiration, below are some stitched examples of the F1 flower. An appliqué design can change dramatically when different color plans and fabrics are used.

(image of F1 flower examples continues below)

Accurate Cutting

After the templates are prepared (pages 20 and 21), they need to be cut out. A template that is accurately cut will lead to a perfect appliqué. Templates with jagged or bumpy edges, points, or overcut details will result in appliqués that don't quite fit properly in the design or, worse yet, leave unwanted gaps between design elements.

> **GATHER:**
> * Scissors
> * Prepared template sheets for F1 flower

 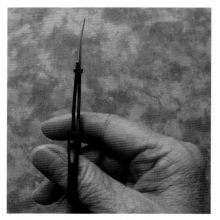 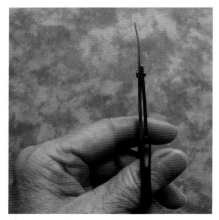

Righty: Curved tip toward the right   *Lefty:* Curved tip toward the left

Using *straight* scissors or *curved-tip* scissors is entirely a matter of personal preference. I prefer curved-tip scissors for template cutting. The recommended way to cut with curved scissors is to point the curved tips toward your cutting hand at all times.

The hand used to hold the scissors is your *cutting hand*. Its job is to open and close the blades of the scissors. For the best control, hold your cutting hand in a stationary position with your arm bent at the elbow (90°), tucked in, and resting beside your waist. This helps to stabilize the cutting hand.

The hand used to hold the paper is your *driving hand*. Its job is to hold and guide the template. For greater control and accuracy, the driving hand is the hand that steers the paper. Your elbow rests at the waist, while the forearm, wrist, and hand are free to twist and turn the paper while cutting.

When cutting, never open and close the blades completely. Try drawing some squiggly lines on paper and practice cutting. Find the sweet spot, located somewhere around the middle of the blades on your scissors. Confine your cutting to that area. NOTE: If you are clipping, you will need to close the points all the way.

Work to coordinate your driving hand so it maneuvers the cutting line toward the sweet spot, while your cutting hand takes small, cutting bites in the paper. This technique works the same for straight and curved scissors. Both hands work together to negotiate the ins and outs of the template perimeter for smooth, flowing cut profiles.

Don't get discouraged if you feel a bit awkward when you first try this new technique. It won't take long to get the hang of it, and you'll be glad you worked to get it right. Accuracy and speed will follow.

Hands work together to cut out a template.

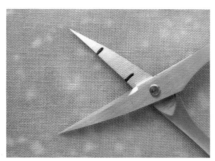

Sweet spot on the scissors blade

 tip *The beauty of templates constructed with freezer paper is that new ones can be made in a jiffy, if needed. Don't be tempted to use a faulty template. Just trace a replacement and you'll have a perfect new one in minutes.*

Cutting Open Templates

Cut out the F1 flower petals and leaf. These templates are *open templates*, meaning the appliqués made from them will have some of their fabric edges turned under, while other edges will not be turned under. The unturned cut areas are open, or left with a raw edge, indicated with zigzag lines on the templates.

For open templates, cut on the solid lines and just along the outside edge of the zigzag lines. Don't cut off the zigzag lines because you'll need to see these critical marks later for cutting out the fabric shapes.

1. Begin to cut from the outside edge of the paper, working around the entire perimeter of the shape. If you are right-handed, it works best to cut from right to left (counterclockwise); lefties work left to right (clockwise). Stop from time to time to readjust your hold on the paper while cutting around the perimeter. Cut along the outer edge of the zigzag markings. NOTE: Keep the template sheet as intact as possible; you'll use it later as a preview window (page 25). **FIGURE A**

2. Evaluate your templates: Are all cut edges crisp and fairly close to the original shape? Are the curves smooth and rounded? Are the corners or points sharp? Is the template sheet intact (as much as possible)?

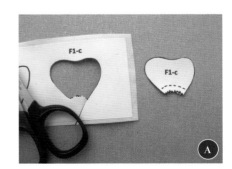

Appliqué Basics

Cutting Closed Templates

The template for the oval F1 flower center is a *closed template,* meaning the appliqué made from it will have all the fabric edges turned under. A closed template will have no raw edges.

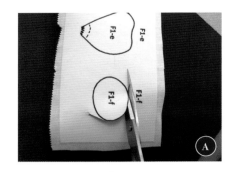

One option for cutting out a closed template is to cut from the outside edge, the same as for the petals. However, I prefer to handle this cut a little differently. I use the point of my scissors to poke a starting hole in the paper. For safety, I recommend working on a hard surface protected by a mouse pad.

1. With the freezer paper template on top of a mouse pad, poke a starting hole, just to the outside of the oval.

2. Hold the template sheet with your driving hand. Insert the bottom blade tip into the hole, making little snips until the slit in the freezer paper is large enough to let you begin cutting around the shape. The bottom blade remains below the freezer paper, while the top scissors blade remains on the surface. **FIGURE A**

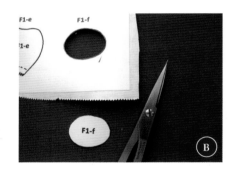

3. Your primary objective is to cut out a precise template, while at the same time causing minimal damage to the remaining freezer paper template sheet. **FIGURE B**

 note *Why so much fuss about cutting templates accurately? First, the quality of fabric appliqué depends on the quality of the template. Second, the freezer paper sheet that remains after the templates have been removed becomes a window for viewing the fabric from which the appliqués will be made. If the window piece keeps springing open, which sometimes happens with larger pieces, use masking tape on the paper side to hold the cut edges together.*

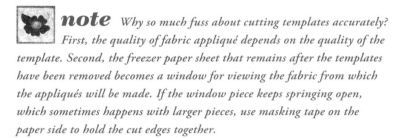 **tip**
Organizing Templates
Use zipper-type plastic bags to store templates and the sheets they are cut from. Label each bag with the name of the pattern and design element.

Simply Successful Appliqué

Window Shopping

Fussy Cutting

Becoming immersed in a new appliqué project can find you addicted to every facet of the process, but there's nothing quite as intriguing as poring over your fabric, searching for the perfect place to cut out each piece. Isolating a very specific area or design in a fabric print and then cutting it out is called *fussy cutting.*

Using the windows from the cut-out freezer paper template sheets allows you to see the exact place in the fabric that will make the most perfect appliqués. No guesswork! But, best of all, the most amazing and unexpected visual surprises can be seen through those windows. In the examples (at right), note the fabric details surrounding each window. Sometimes a leaf in the print is obvious, but other times it isn't. Look how easy it becomes by using a window.

Use the following method, and your appliqué fabric piece will turn out exactly as it is viewed within the window opening.

GATHER:

- Zipper bag (containing prepared freezer paper templates and windows)
- Hard pressing board
- Iron
- Iron rest
- Fabric
- Scissors (preferably 4″ straight scissors for cutting fabric)

PREPARE:

Set iron on cotton/linen, dry—no steam. Press out any wrinkles in the fabric, if necessary.

1. Arrange windows and templates in pairs. **FIGURE A**

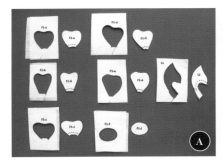
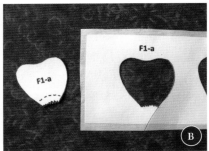

2. On the pressing board, spread out the selected fabric, smoothing it out by hand. Use the template window to pinpoint your fabric choice. When you find a perfect petal peering up at you through that window, heat press the template window securely to the fabric with a hot, dry iron. The fabric showing up through the window will look exactly the same when the fabric appliqué piece is finished and sewn to your block. **FIGURE B**

tip *If you decide you're not happy with the results of your window shopping, simply peel the freezer paper window off the fabric and begin again.*

3. Insert the template inside the window opening. Press with the iron to adhere the template to the fabric. **FIGURE C**

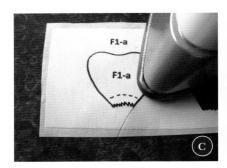

4. Peel off only the template window, leaving the template affixed to the fabric. Check to make certain none of the template edges have been lifted while the template sheet was being removed. If so, press the template again with the iron to secure all edges to the fabric.

5. Lift the fabric from the pressing board. Use your hand beneath the fabric to help poke a starting hole on the fabric surface using the bottom point of the scissors. **FIGURE D**

6. Cut around the template, leaving a ⅛″ seam allowance next to the solid lines. Cut just to the outside edge of any zigzag lines. NOTE: Righties will cut counter-clockwise around the templates; lefties will work clockwise.

7. Window shop and cut the fabric pieces for all remaining templates. **FIGURES E–G**

Surprise Cut Pieces

You'll be so excited about using windows you'll forget that many times it's not necessary to go through the window-shopping process. The fabric may be a blender or tiny allover print, or you may want to enjoy the thrill of being surprised. In these instances, simply iron the freezer paper templates onto the fabric (anywhere they land), and then cut them out with a ⅛″ seam allowance.

Seam Allowances

Many methods for turned-edge appliqué recommend cutting a full ¼″ seam allowance around the edges of templates. But with Simply Successful Appliqué techniques, it isn't necessary to add all that fabric bulk in the seams.

You'll be able to control all potential for fraying, so only ⅛″ is recommended for most seam allowances. The exceptions are that when working with very tiny shapes or tightly woven fabrics, such as batiks, a scant (narrower) ⅛″ seam can be used; and for meatier, looser-weave fabrics, a fat (tad wider) ⅛″ works best.

It's important for you to get a good idea in your mind's eye about what an actual ⅛″ looks like. Take a moment to study a ruler so you can fix the width of ⅛″ in your memory. Like most new skills, your accuracy will improve just by doing it, so don't overthink this. Don't worry about marking cutting lines—just eye it. Experience will be its own reward.

Each small square on this Omnigrid ruler is ⅛″ wide × ⅛″ long. Try to commit ⅛″ to memory.

Making Preturned Appliqués

You've color planned and selected fabric, window shopped and cut out pieces, so you should have a pretty good idea by now of what your project will look like. Right? Well, hold on to your hat, because this last step in preparing the appliqués is part of what makes Simply Successful Appliqué so, well, simply successful! No matter what you've got pictured in your mind, when you begin to turn under the fabric edges and watch those scraps transform into petals and leaves, the delightful results promise to exceed all expectation!

In this section, you'll learn the essential steps for turning and stabilizing appliqué seam allowances prior to stitching. Hands down, it's the easiest, quickest, and all-around best way to prepare turned-edge appliqué!

GATHER:
- Paintbrush
- Glass bowl
- Sizing
- Awl (*or* stiletto *or* long pearl-head pin)
- Iron
- Hard pressing board

PREPARE:
Set your iron to dry cotton/linen, no steam.

note *Throughout the instructions,* wet *means to wet with sizing;* press *or* heat set *means to press with a hot, dry iron.*

Preparing Appliqués with Basic Shapes

Preturning a Basic Petal Shape

1. Spray sizing in a small bowl. Sizing is foamy when it's first sprayed from an aerosol can but turns to liquid after a few minutes.

2. Begin with a fabric cutout with the template on top. **FIGURE A**

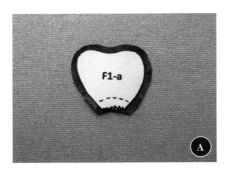

3. Peel the freezer paper template off the fabric, turn the fabric cutout *wrong side up*, and center the template *shiny side up* on top of the fabric. **FIGURE B**

4. With a hot, dry iron, press the fabric seam allowances over the edges of the freezer paper. The fabric will adhere to the shiny plastic side of the template. The double layer of freezer paper makes the template edges strong and rigid so the original shape is maintained while the iron manipulates the fabric. Right-handers should begin on the right-hand side and work counterclockwise with the iron; lefties begin on the left-hand side and work clockwise. The following directions are given for righties. Lefties are kindly asked to mirror the process.

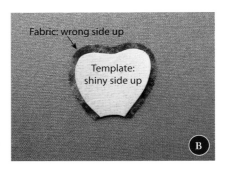

Fabric: wrong side up

Template: shiny side up

For turning fabric edges, the movement of the iron can best be described as a circular sideswipe. The tip of the iron enters from the right, grabbing and lifting the fabric from beneath the right edge. As the fabric folds over the template edge, sweep the iron tip to the left and downward in a little arc. You'll get the hang of it in just a few swipes. Move up the right-hand side of the template, continuing to roll the fabric over the template edges. **FIGURE C**

 tip
Centering and Stabilizing Fabric on a Template
It's easiest to keep the template centered on top of the fabric by holding it down with the left thumb while the fabric edge is turned over with the iron (using the right hand). Start by turning a small area on the right-hand side of the shape, then a small area on the left-hand side, and then a small area (or two) in between. This **heat-tacking** *approach stabilizes the template in the center of the fabric, freeing up your hands to use a pointed tool to help ease in fabric fullness, where necessary.*

5. Rotate the shape and begin to roll the fabric over the template edge on the other side; heat press to adhere. This keeps the template centered on the fabric without distortion. **FIGURE D**

6. Press the seam allowances over the template edges further up on each side of the petal. To stabilize the top center area of the shape, use the tip of the iron to turn over the fabric, hugging the contour of the freezer paper template. Take note of how the iron is perpendicular to the edge being worked on—use your left hand to continually readjust the template position while your right hand drives the iron tip, coming in at a right angle to the edge being pressed. **FIGURE E**

7. Look closely now at the petal's unturned corner areas. Focus on a corner at a time. A lot of fabric needs to be eased into a small area inside the perimeter of the shape. You will need an awl (or other pointed tool) to help distribute the excess fabric into small gathers. Just dip the tip of the paintbrush into the liquid sizing and apply it along the edge of the fabric that needs gathering. Be careful not to wet the paper template. **FIGURE F**

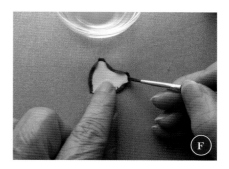

8. Use the point of the awl to fold fabric up and over the template edges in small increments, easing the fabric into tiny gathers. Use your left thumb to hold the gathers as the tool draws in the fabric. Each time a little gather is formed, hold it down with the tip of your thumb as you work to shape the next tiny gather. When the tip of your thumb is unable to hold more gathers, put down the tool and pick up the iron. **FIGURE G**

9. Use the iron tip to press the area until it is dry. If needed, pick up the awl again and continue to gather the remaining edge fabric, heat pressing the corner to set the gathered turned edges. **FIGURE H**

10. Repeat for the remaining corner.

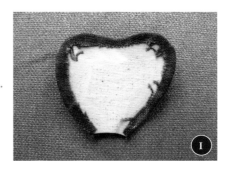

11. Press each corner section again, with the iron tip until the sizing is dry and the fabric adheres to the template. The sizing acts like an adhesive, giving the tiny folds in the fabric a memory and helping them adhere to the edges of the freezer paper template. **FIGURE I**

Learning by Doing: Skills Learned by Preturning a Petal Appliqué

The flower motif, while simple, is designed to include many of the common line and shape elements that you will encounter in most appliqué designs. By making flower petals, you've been introduced to straight lines (along the sides of some of the petals), outside curves (the petal corners and some of the petal sides), and gentle inside U curves (the dip in the center of the flower petals, between their two corners).

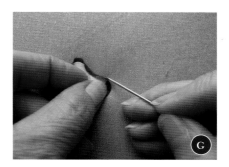

Resizing Edges

Resizing the folded edges of a preturned appliqué is precautionary. When the freezer paper template is removed from the fabric, the seam allowance will be stressed slightly. Resizing and pressing the edges can help more vulnerable areas of fabric (those with a tendency to fray) to remain crisp at the edges. Resizing is also discretionary. When needed, the sizing adds light body without stiffness, and you'll be happy for the way it keeps the appliqués in pristine condition until they are used.

1. With a piece wrong side up, apply sizing along the folded edges in small increments.

2. Press the resized edges until they are dry.

3. Turn the appliqué to the front side and apply sizing to the raw, unturned edge; press to dry. **FIGURE A**

tip *Leave the fabric adhered to the freezer paper template until just before you're ready to sew. Removing the fabric beforehand increases the risk of having the edges fray. In time, the fibers absorb humidity, and even though the edges have been sized, the fold crease will begin to relax and will no longer be as sharp.*

Preturning a Basic Leaf Shape

This is the step-by-step guide for making a preturned leaf appliqué. Many lessons can be learned from this seemingly straightforward shape, not the least of which is how to make the world's most perfect pointy point! The leaf (like a petal) is made using an open template.

1. Begin with a fabric cutout with the template on top. **FIGURE B**

2. Peel the freezer paper template off the fabric, turn the fabric *wrong side up,* and center the template *shiny side up* on top of the fabric. **FIGURE C**

3. Heat tack the edges (left and right sides) to stabilize. This will ensure sufficient fabric for the turnover on each side of the leaf tip. **FIGURE D**

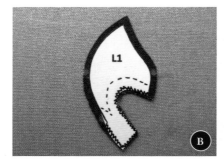

4. Continue to turn the fabric over the template edge. The fabric extends past the freezer paper template in a smooth, continuous curve, forming a fabric flag at the tip. **FIGURE E**

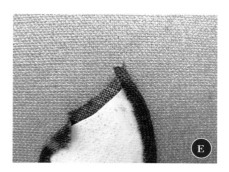

5. The fabric is adhered to the freezer paper up to the point where it goes beyond the template edge. The fabric at the tip will be folded onto fabric, to which it will *not* adhere. A dab of sizing will glue the 2 fabric surfaces together temporarily when heat set. This makes them stable and immune to fraying. This also stiffens the fabric, making it easier to turn the second side of the leaf tip. You can tell where sizing has been applied because the fabric appears darker. Press the leaf tip to adhere the fabric layers. **FIGURE F**

6. Turn the leaf tip to face toward you. Apply sizing to the tip again.

7. Use your left thumbnail to hold down the tip while using an awl (with the right hand) to fold the flag back onto itself, making a sharp crease at the turned edge; heat press. The flag will extend beyond the edge profile. Turn and press all the remaining fabric edges, making sure they are smooth. **FIGURE G**

note *Do not* under any circumstances *be tempted to cut off the excess fabric from a leaf tip flag! Cutting the nearby fabric destroys the weave structure, letting threads work their way loose at the point when you stitch it.*

8. To tame those ragged flag edges without cutting: Turn the leaf tip away from you. The flag needs to turn back on itself again. Apply sizing to the protruding fabric on the tip.

9. Hold down the piece with your left thumb and thumbnail while using an awl in your right hand to fold the flag back onto the leaf tip. Use an awl point to hold down the flag. Keep pressure on the flag with the tip of the iron, slipping the awl point out from beneath. Continue to press the leaf tip until dry. **FIGURE H**

tip *Don't be nosy and peek under the iron until you've given it a chance to dry the fabric, but be careful not to scorch it. If you're not happy with the tip, then just rewet it, reshape it, and re-iron it. You can work on it until you get it just right.*

10. On the back side of the piece, reapply sizing in small increments to the folded-edge creases, pressing as you go.

11. Flip the leaf to the right side to apply sizing to the raw edge and press. The leaf is prepped and ready for stitching. **FIGURE I**

Preturning a Basic Oval or Circle Shape

The F1 sampler flower has an oval center. An oval uses a closed template, meaning all the edges are turned under. There are no open areas with raw edges.

1. Begin with a fabric cutout with the template on top. Peel the freezer paper template off the fabric, turn the fabric *wrong side up,* and center the template *shiny side up* on top of the fabric.

2. Stabilize the fabric by first turning the edges on 2 opposing sides and heat pressing them onto the shiny side of the freezer paper. One side at a time, apply sizing to the unturned fabric edges. **FIGURE A**

3. Coax the fabric fullness into tiny gathers on the sides of the oval; heat press to secure. **FIGURE B**

4. On the completed oval, all the edges have been resized and pressed dry. Remember: If you're unhappy with any of the turned edges, it's easy to go back now and fix them. **FIGURES C–D**

Troubleshooting: Appliqués with Unwelcome Peaks or Other Flaws

If you notice an unwelcome bulge or peak anywhere on the turned edge of an appliqué piece *at any time,* it's not too late to fix it!

1. The right edge of this appliqué petal has a peak, rather than a smooth curve. The time to fix it easily is right now, as soon as you notice it! Don't wait until you're stitching, when you'll need to struggle to correct it. Checking your prepared appliqué pieces from the front side is a good habit to get into. **FIGURE E**

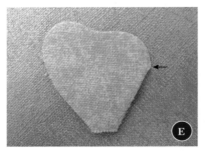

2. For a quick fix, rewet the flawed area with sizing. This will relax the fabric, and it will begin to loosen from the freezer paper. Use an awl point to gently release the fabric edge from the template. **FIGURE F**

3. Roll the fabric over the edge of the template with the iron to correct the problem. Heat set. Check the front of the appliqué to see the reworked edge details. Perfect! **FIGURE G**

Preturning Appliqués with Other Shapes: Some Simple, Some Complex

We've covered a lot of territory in the preparation of appliqué pieces. Now on to other shapes: some basic and some more challenging. These elements go beyond the sampler project, expanding your comfort zone by familiarizing you with additional patch preparation.

A primary teaching objective for this book is to eliminate the fear factor by providing you with the tools and strategies that will give you confidence to make any appliqué project you set your sights on. With your appliqué bag filled with Simply Successful Appliqué tips and tricks, you'll develop a sophisticated eye for analyzing the most intricate designs, seeing that they are all essentially made up of the same basic shapes you'll find here.

Guidelines for Preturning Appliqué Seam Allowances

- If you hear a loud sizzle when the iron touches the fabric, the iron is too hot. A very faint sizzle is fine. If you see areas of residual white (or scorched) sizing remaining on the surface of the fabric or iron soleplate, you may have used too much sizing or not allowed it enough time to be absorbed by the fabric.

- If the template edges are crushing in, distorting the shape of the appliqué, try a gentler approach when using the iron tip to coax the fabric over and onto the freezer paper. Another culprit might be too much sizing, which can soften the template edges or release the fabric from the template edges. Try using less sizing.

- If you are having difficulty turning edges, it might have nothing to do with you or the sizing or your ironing skills; but rather, it might be that the freezer paper you're working with is too thin. Just fuse a third layer of freezer paper to your templates. They will be heavier and thicker, and your problem should be solved.

- Above all, make certain you're working on a hard pressing surface!

Preturning Wide Appliqués with Straight Edges

Sunflower Glory (page 123), in progress. The vase rim is a wide, straight-edged appliqué.

1. Cut the appliqué fabric ⅛″ beyond the template edges, with the raw edges trimmed even with the zigzags on the template. **FIGURE A**

2. Peel the freezer paper template off the fabric, turn the fabric *wrong side up,* and center the template *shiny side up* on top of the fabric. Heat tack to stabilize the position of the template on the fabric. **FIGURE B**

3. Turn over the seam allowances along the length of a side, heat pressing the fabric onto the freezer paper. **FIGURE C**

4. Rotate the piece and turn over the seam allowance, heat pressing the remaining side edges. **FIGURES D–E**

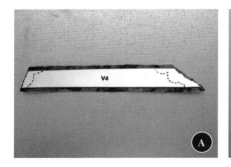

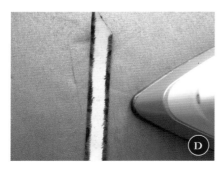

Preturning Narrow Appliqués with Straight Edges

The sunflower stem is a narrow, straight-edged appliqué, only ¼″ wide. (See Double-Double Pressed Skinny Stems, pages 104 and 105, for another way to make stems.)

1. Prepare and cut out the stem. Peel the freezer paper template off the fabric, turn the fabric *wrong side up,* and center the template *shiny side up* on top of the fabric. Heat tack to stabilize the template in position. **FIGURE F**

2. Turn the seam allowance along the entire length of an edge. Wet the edge with sizing and heat set. **FIGURE G**

3. Rotate the stem and wet it along the entire length. (The unturned edge must be wet prior to turning because fabric will not stick to fabric without sizing.) Fold over and heat set the second side edge. **FIGURES H–I**

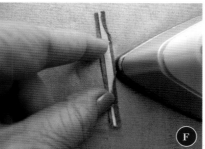

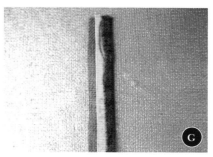

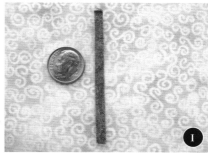

Completed preturned narrow, straight-edged appliqué

Preturning Tiny Appliqués

Sunflower Glory (page 123) has tiny leaves.

Working with very small appliqué pieces can be challenging, but below are a few tips to make it easier:

- If you're working with small pieces, you'll find it helpful to rely more on pointed tools to help manipulate the fabric. Smaller pieces have less area to hold on to, and you'll obviously need to keep your fingertips away from the hot iron. An awl, a long pearl-head pin, or a sharp scissors point can safely step in when your fingers can't get close. If an appliqué is really tiny, use two awls, one in each hand: one to hold and one to fold.

- Fraying can be a problem with small appliqués. If after cutting out a small patch you notice fraying edges, stabilize the edges.

1. Peel off the template and wet the fabric edges. **FIGURE A**

2. Heat press, stabilizing the edges, and then proceed as usual to turn the edges of the appliqué.

note *If you are making appliqué pieces with points, such as leaves, be sure to rewet and heat set the fabric flags at the tips to make them stiff (page 31). The flag will then turn over easily for a sharp point.*

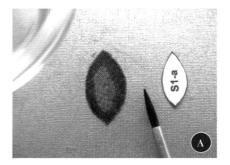

Preturning Appliqués with Narrow Outside Curves, Narrow Inside U Curves, and Narrow Oval Reverse Appliqué

This featured appliqué shape has been selected because it requires several preparation techniques to complete, making it a great teaching motif. You'll often come across an appliqué shape with a narrow outside curve or one with a narrow inside U, and on occasion, you'll want to add a reverse appliqué element for a special touch. This flower has it all in one!

Appearing in *Tweet Treats* (page 123), this stylized flower features narrow outside curves at the top corners with a deep well between them. The red elongated oval in the center of the flower has been treated as a reverse appliqué, with a different fabric showing through the opening. NOTE: The following instructions show how the appliqué for just the body of this flower is constructed. The red bud at the tip is a separate appliqué piece with a narrow outside curve.

1. Cut out the F2-b template. **FIGURE B**

2. To cut a slim, elongated inside oval, fold the template in half. Cut a starting slit in the center. **FIGURE C**

3. Working from underneath, bring the top blade of the scissors up through the starting slit. Cut out the center oval. Taking little snips with the scissor points helps to turn the tight curve. **FIGURE D**

4. Heat press the template onto the *right* side of the fabric. Cut around the template, leaving a ⅛″ seam allowance. **FIGURE E**

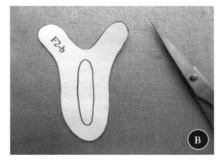

B

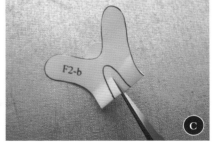

C

D

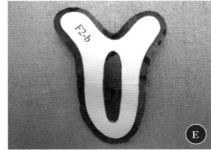

E

5. Peel off the template. Referring to Preturning a Basic Petal Shape (pages 28–30), turn the edges and stabilize the template on the outside and at the sides of the well. **FIGURE F**

Narrow Outside Curves

1. Wet a curved tip. Gather in the fullness with an awl. **FIGURE G**

2. Heat set. Repeat the process on the other curved tip. **FIGURE H**

Narrow Inside U

1. Clip the fabric once to within 3 or 4 threads of cutting into the template edge in the well center between the flower tips. This is a deep U. The fabric will not stretch or give enough to fold around the deep contour of this shape. So, in this rare instance, the center needs to be clipped. **FIGURE I**

2. Wet the well area of the fabric edge. A little more stretch is possible with wet fabric. Experience will teach you that in these deep U shapes, both clipping and sizing are needed to help encourage the fabric to stretch around the deep inside curve.

3. Turn the edges. Notice the angle of the iron tip: the iron is lifted off the pressing board (with handle tilted away) so the iron tip can reach in to roll over the edges inside the well. The sizing helps to heat set the fabric to the inside curve of the template. **FIGURE J**

4. Look closely at the well center. You can see how the fabric has split at the point where it was clipped. The clip and sizing allowed the surrounding weave to relax so it could be molded to the profile of the template. Notice also that the very center of the well still has intact fabric rolled over onto the freezer paper. This area will require a delicate touch when removing the freezer paper before it is stitched down, but its weave structure is stable. Resizing this fragile area will provide an extra ounce of prevention (see Resizing Edges, page 30). **FIGURE K**

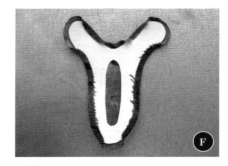

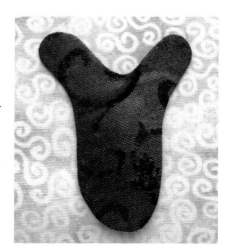

Options: One way to interpret this flower is to use it as is, with a solid center. Alternatively, the oval that was cut from the freezer paper template can serve as a template for making a long oval appliqué to be layered on top of the flower body. A third option for interpreting this flower is to use reverse appliqué for the long oval design element.

Narrow Oval Reverse Appliqué

1. With the piece facing wrong side up, cut a slit in the center of the long oval. Take care not to cut too near the template edges at each end, leaving 3 or 4 woven threads intact. **FIGURE L**

2. Heat tack the left inside edge of the oval. Use the tilted tip of the iron to heat set the remaining length of the edge, but do not go too near the top or bottom of the oval for now (this could disturb the fragile weave in those areas). **FIGURE M**

3. Using the iron, turn the edge on the remaining side of the oval. With both side edges stabilized, wet the bottom U of the oval. First, lift the piece and use the shaft of the awl to coax the wet fabric to roll forward and over onto the template edge, pulling the back to the front through the template opening. Then, place the template on a flat surface and use the point of the awl to manipulate the fabric over the template edges. **FIGURE N**

4. Lift the piece again, using a paintbrush handle to roll the fabric edges forward. Because the fabric edges are wet and relaxed, they will spread out and turn over onto the freezer paper template. At the endpoints of the oval, only a few woven threads are left intact, but that's all you need. A brush handle works in this case because the oval opening closely matches the diameter of this brush handle. At other times, a knitting needle, round pencil, or skewer might match the element you're working on. Be creative in looking for objects that can serve as turning tools. **FIGURE O**

5. With a tilted, downturned iron tip, target the narrow U inside the oval and heat set the turned edges. Rotate the appliqué and repeat the steps for the top of the oval. **FIGURES P–Q**

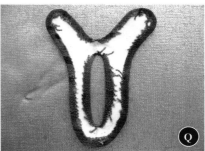

tip
Reminder!

Resize and heat set any areas that could be in jeopardy. This extra step is preemptive, serving to further reinforce the weave structure in vulnerable areas and making template removal less invasive when it comes time to sew.

Preturning Deep Inside V Shapes

A Basketful of Hope (page 124) features shallow V and deep V design elements.

Another common design element is an inside V. This is found at the top midsection of a heart, for example. In *A Basketful of Hope,* curves and shallow V shapes form the bottom edge of the basket. Most often, V shapes are fairly shallow, but I've chosen a more challenging deep V appliqué piece for this example. After successfully making a very deep V with Simply Successful Appliqué, making a shallow V will be a cakewalk for you! You are always free to adjust any pattern by redrawing the lines. For example, you may wish to redraw ribbon tails to make a V shallow and technically less challenging. But do give the deep V a try. Taking it step by step, you may very well be surprised at how easy it can be to make a deep V!

1. Refer to Preparing Appliqués with Basic Shapes (pages 28–32) to prepare the appliqué and turn the edges until you get to the deep V at the center of the ribbon tail.

2. Clip the fabric inside the deep V to within 2 or 3 threads of touching the template paper. Your goal is to leave an even amount of fabric on the left and the right sides of the cut. **FIGURE A**

3. Wet inside the V and each point. **FIGURE B**

4. Heat set the center clipped area and the 2 ribbon tail points, stabilizing the fabric weave in these areas.

5. With the ribbon points facing toward you, rewet the left point. Fold over the seam allowance back onto the point, using an awl. Handle the ribbon points the same as you would an appliqué leaf point (page 31). **FIGURE C**

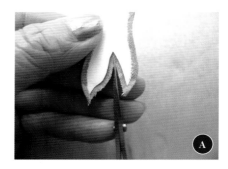

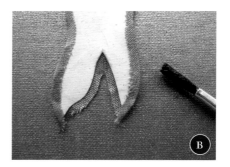

6. Keeping a firm pressure on the awl with your left hand, heat set the left ribbon point. **FIGURE D**

7. Notice that no flag was formed on this point. This is a rare occasion when all excess fabric and stray threads are stabilized in a single shot. This doesn't happen often. If a flag is present, resize the point, tuck in those strays, and heat press again. Notice that I have turned more fabric along the inside edge of the ribbon's point. **FIGURE E**

8. This is a great little trick: To reach inside the deep V, slide your iron in from underneath the opposite ribbon tip to heat press the turn allowance. The freezer paper is flexible so it can be bent up and out of the way temporarily. **FIGURE F**

9. The inside edge of the first ribbon point is turned under. NOTE: Do not attempt to go further inside the V for now. If you look closely, you can see that a bit of fabric nearest the center of the V has not yet been turned. **FIGURE G**

10. On the second ribbon point, wet the flag, fold over the fabric, and press to form the point. Ignore the flag at the tip for now. **FIGURE H**

11. To heat set the inside edge, slide the iron underneath the opposite point. **FIGURE I**

12. Wet the fabric inside the V. Use the awl point and shaft to pull the fabric forward, rolling it over the template edge. Hold any stray threads down with your thumbnail or awl. Heat set with the tilted iron tip. If necessary, rewet the V to coax any additional stray threads of fabric toward the shiny side of the template. Heat set. Repeat as necessary until you're happy with the results. **FIGURE J**

13. Return to the left ribbon flag. Wet, fold over, and heat press. Rework as necessary, tucking in all stray threads on the ribbon point. **FIGURES K–L**

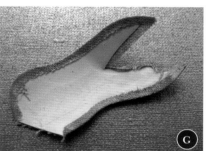

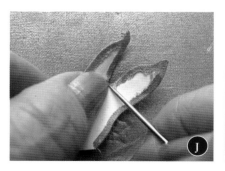

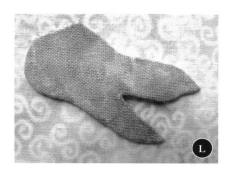

Preturning Rings

Circles within circles, or rings, are common design elements. They look simple enough, but because their edges are on the bias, it can be especially challenging to ensure that they stay round. Some Simply Successful Appliqué tricks will make it easy!

Hugs 'n' Kisses (page 122) features an appliqué ring surrounding the central heart motif.

1. Start with a square piece of fabric that's larger than the ring. Prepare and mark a ring template with registration marks (*N, S, E,* and *W*) on the template and the outside freezer paper window. After window shopping (pages 25 and 26), match up registration marks to align and insert the template. Heat set the template in place on the fabric. **FIGURE A**

2. Remove the outside window. **FIGURE B**

3. Cut around the template, leaving a ⅛″ fabric turn-under seam allowance. NOTE: Mark a ↑N↑ (for north) on the back *and* front sides of the fabric seam allowance. **FIGURE C**

4. Peel off the template. Draw an arrow on the *shiny* side of the template (look on the paper side of the template for the arrow placement). Flip the template and fabric over. **FIGURE D**

5. Center the fabric and template. Heat tack in place. **FIGURE E**

6. In small increments, turn all edges and heat press, using an awl to gather the edges, reinforcing them with sizing as necessary. Completing the outer edges of

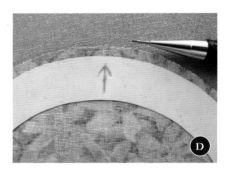

a ring first will stabilize the entire perimeter with the round shape held true. Preturning the ring's inside edges then becomes a straightforward process, without the fabric or template shape skewing.

7. To cut the seam allowance for the inner edge of the ring, poke a starting hole with the scissors. From beneath, use the top point of the scissors to cut around the inside ring curve, leaving a ⅛″ turned-edge seam allowance. **FIGURE F**

8. Remove the excess center fabric. Lifting the top edge of the ring, insert the iron tip (from behind) to heat tack the turned edges at the *N, S, E,* and *W* locations. **FIGURE G**

9. The inside edges will need to be stretched around the inside curve as they are turned onto the template. Apply sizing to the fabric edges to encourage stretching. This should eliminate any need to clip the inside curved edges. Use the iron tip to coax, turn, and heat set all edges onto the template. **FIGURE H**

10. Resize and heat set all the ring edges. **FIGURE I**

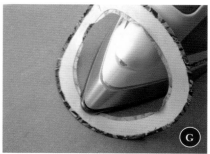

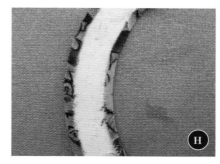

Organizing Prepared Appliqués

Just as planning is required to stay organized when using templates and windows, you'll find it helpful to arrange appliqués in a way that will keep them safe and make them easy to identify. You'll especially appreciate this as you begin to sew pieces onto the background.

GATHER:
- 3 copies of master pattern
- Pattern overlay
- Tweezers
- Prepared appliqué pieces
- Tweezers

Plan to use one copy of the master pattern as a visual reference for the composition as a whole. You'll find yourself referring to it often. A second copy, along with tweezers, can sit at arm's length by the side of your work area. As you prepare a fabric appliqué, use tweezers to place it on top of its designated space. A third copy can be used as a working copy when you are ready to stitch, transferring a few appliqués at a time so you won't disturb the layout on the second copy.

Auditioning Appliqués on a Background

Audition the background fabric to see exactly how your appliqués will relate before stitching! Place the overlay onto the background fabric. Place preturned appliqués on top of the overlay. If things don't appear the way you want, it's easy to make adjustments.

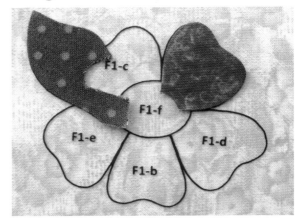

Removing Paper Templates

- A preturned appliqué piece should remain fixed to its template until you are ready to stitch it down.

GATHER:
- Lapboard
- Awl
- Tweezers
- Prepared appliqué pieces

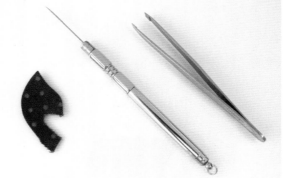

- To begin, select the first appliqué piece that will be stitched to the background fabric. For the F1 flower, this is the L1 leaf because it sits behind the flower petals. The freezer paper template will need to be removed from inside the fabric appliqué before sewing.

- Use a lapboard for releasing the freezer paper. A lapboard will also make an easier job of pin-basting or glue-basting appliqués in place on the background. If you don't have a lapboard, use an alternative hard surface that will not be harmed by an awl, pins, or glue.

- My lapboard is made of Plexiglas and is transparent. In the following illustrations, it is resting on my lap and my hands are working on the board. I wore a white skirt so the appliqués would show up clearly in contrast.

Releasing Fabric Edges from Templates

1. Place the appliqué facedown on the lapboard, stabilizing it with your left index finger. To separate the paper template from the fabric, move the awl point back and forth along the turned edge in small increments. Angle the awl horizontally, putting pressure on the point to wedge it between the fabric and the paper.
FIGURE A

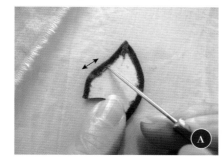

2. By pressing onto the paper, you can release the fabric without putting stress on its weave structure. If you hold the awl low, the point will bear down on the paper rather than scrape up on the underside of the fabric. **FIGURE B**

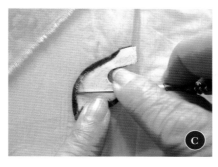 

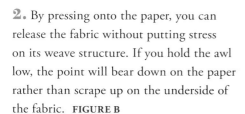 ***tip*** *When separating the fabric from the template, keep the tool point from penetrating too near the edge fold of the appliqué so the edge crease stays sharp.*

3. Rotate the appliqué, working around the perimeter of the shape. **FIGURE C**

4. In general, work your way around an appliqué shape by first separating the wider curves and then last releasing the fabric gently from any fragile areas, narrow points, or deep inside V shapes. **FIGURE D**

Removing Template Paper

1. To preserve any fragile areas, such as the sharp point on this leaf, pinch the fragile area with your left hand using your thumb and index finger. Pick up the tweezers with your right hand, inserting its lower leg between the fabric and the template paper (at the base of the leaf). Pinch the tweezers closed, grabbing the paper only. **FIGURE E**

2. Twist the tweezers to the left to pop the template out of the preturned fabric fold on the right seam. **FIGURE F**

3. Continue pinching any fragile areas, twisting tweezers to the right, to release the paper from its left seam. Keep pinching the fragile area. A slight tug now on the template paper will release it the rest of the way. Removing the template in this way will cause the least amount of distortion to the fabric shape, minimizing disruption to the edge weave. **FIGURE G**

4. With the template removed, all preturned fabric edges are in perfect condition. The shape is true to its original pattern outline. **FIGURE H**

tip
Reminder!

Remove the template from its fabric appliqué just before you're ready to pin-baste or glue-baste it to the background for stitching. Humidity in the air can quickly relax the sharp fold, and it will be easier to stitch if the edge remains crisp. Work with one piece at a time.

Using an Overlay to Position Appliqués

When using an overlay (pages 17 and 18), there is no need to trace or transfer the design lines onto the background fabric. An overlay ensures the exact placement of all the appliqués, no matter how many pieces or how many layers will be stitched down to complete the design. The larger or more complex the design, the more valuable this placement method will become to you. NOTE: If you've previously used an overlay and it did not work for you, please try again, using the following guidelines.

To review: Registration marks (*N, S, E, W*, with ↑N↑ highlighted) are added to the master pattern, the overlay, and the background fabric.

Aligning Registration Marks

Plan for a workspace with a comfortable chair where you can sit up straight. Your tools, prepared background block (pages 13–16), and appliqués should be conveniently within reach.

Place the background fabric right side up on the lapboard. Smooth the fabric flat. Place the overlay on top of the fabric, matching up all the registration marks on the fabric and the overlay. Remember that ↑N↑ indicates the top of the overlay and the tailor's tack stitch marks the top of the background fabric (see photos at top of next page).

GATHER:
- Lapboard
- Pattern overlay
- Background block
- Tweezers
- Awl, stiletto, or long pearl-head pin
- Prepared appliqués

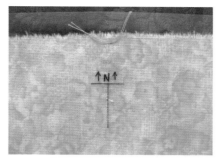
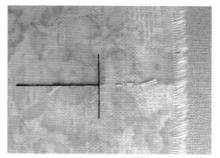

The overlay registration mark (in black) lines up perfectly with the yellow thread basting line on the fabric block.

 tip _To make sure that that the overlay doesn't get flipped, write_ THIS SIDE UP _along the top edge in permanent marker._

Placing Appliqués

1. With all registration marks aligned, place your left hand across the top edge of the overlay, holding it comfortably but firmly in position. With your right hand, slip the first appliqué beneath the overlay and place it in position on the background. Be precise. **FIGURE A**

2. Remove your hand from beneath the overlay. Recheck the registration marks and the appliqué for accurate placement, adjusting as necessary. When satisfied, remove the overlay with both hands. **FIGURE B**

Understanding and Using an Overlay

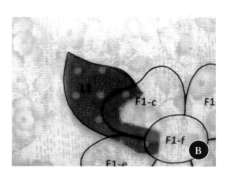

- The overlay is an absolute guide for appliqué placement. It starts out being exact and it will end up being exact. If there is a discrepancy when the overlay is placed on top of the background fabric, it is due to a change in the fabric and not the overlay.

- A discrepancy in matching up the overlay and background will occur when a piece is pinned onto the background. The discrepancy will self-correct when the pins are removed. A discrepancy will also occur when a piece is sewn onto the background. Appliqué stitches make the background fabric draw in (shrink) a little as each piece is sewn. That's why, over the course of a project, the background block will end up measuring less than the square you began with. This is a predictable consequence of sewing on an appliqué. As more and more pieces are sewn on, the fabric will be drawn in more and more (in tiny increments).

- If you have tried using an overlay but haven't been successful, it is not the overlay or the method or you! Instead, the overlay has been used in the wrong way. Read on.

- To this point, you've been told that *all* the registration marks on the background need to line up with the overlay. There is, however, an important exception. As pieces are added and the overlay begins to be discrepant, ignore the *whole* overlay, instead using only one *quadrant* at a time (the overlay quadrant where your piece appears). So, for example, if you want to place a piece in the northeast corner of the block, match up only the *N* and *E* registration lines of the background and overlay. The piece will be placed perfectly!

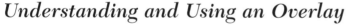

- Discrepancies will be barely noticeable when you're working on basic appliqué designs as in the *Just for Pretty* (page 123) sampler blocks or *Hugs 'n' Kisses* (page 122). More intricate appliqué designs will require you to use overlay quadrants for aligning the pieces.

- Discrepancies between the background and the overlay (even with elaborate designs) can be minimized by soft pressing (pages 92–94) the background from time to time. When I was working on *Springtime's Promise* (page 125), I needed to soft press the background three times (over the course of completing the block) to keep it aligned with the overlay. Another way to minimize discrepancies is to plan your appliqué by scattering the pieces: Sew some pieces in the southwest quadrant and then some in the southeast quadrant, and so on.

Basting Appliqués in Place

Basting temporarily fastens an appliqué piece to the background so it stays in place while it is being stitched down permanently. Pinning and gluing are both fast and accurate methods for basting.

A third basting option—basting with needle and thread—uses running stitches around the perimeter of the appliqué shape. However, before the basting stitches can be sewn, the piece needs to be pinned or glued in place. I could be wrong, but it seems to me that this is double the work. My recommendation is that you pin-baste or glue-baste your appliqués, depending on the task. The following will offer some guidelines.

Pin-Basting

Accurate pinning is a critical, but often overlooked, skill. If pins are not placed properly, the layers of fabric will move (sometimes imperceptibly) before you begin to sew. Using this precision pinning technique can make all the difference, especially when working on multiple layers of appliqués, which appear in complex designs. A little shifting here and there can end up causing big problems.

GATHER:
- Pincushion
- Sequin pins
- Lapboard

---

 tip *It's well worth the effort to learn how to manage ½" sequin pins for pin-basting appliqués. You owe it to yourself to get control of these tiny tools as soon as you can. You get a temporary reprieve if you want to start with the ¾" pearl-head pins, but just until you get the hang of it. You'll thank me for it!*

Advantages of using ½" sequin pins:

- *They're very sharp and thin.*

- *They have a way of nestling themselves nicely into the fabric so that thread rarely, if ever, gets caught up on them.*

- *They hold even small appliqués in place without shifting.*

For *hand* appliqué, *pin-basting* is done by inserting the pins in the same direction that the sewing will be done. For righties, pins are inserted beginning on the right side of the appliqué, working counter-clockwise (the direction in which righties will sew hand stitches). Lefties will begin pinning on the left side of an appliqué, working clockwise (the direction in which lefties will sew hand stitches).

For *machine* appliqué, *pin-basting* is done by placing a few pins (around the center) to stabilize the piece temporarily while the edges are *glue-basted* (page 51). The pins are always removed before sewing.

1. Working on a lapboard, begin at the right side of the appliqué. Hold the appliqué on the background with your left hand. With your right hand, grab a pin head. Point the pin straight down (perpendicular to the lapboard surface), aiming just inside the turned edge fold. The idea is to dive vertically, straight down into the surface of the appliqué and through the background fabric. I call this "dive-bombing." It's a stabbing motion that ensures that the pinpoint is inserted straight down through all the fabric layers, stopping when it hits the lapboard. This method prevents the appliqué and background fabric from shifting out of position. **FIGURE A**

2. When the pinpoint touches the lapboard surface, tilt the pin head toward the right while pushing the point toward the left. The point remains beneath background fabric as it travels about ¼″. **FIGURE B**

3. Continue to hold the appliqué in place with your left hand. Use your right hand to push the pin, taking a scoop or bite of the fabric, with the point reemerging on the appliqué surface. Use your pin-pushing fingers and pin-receiving finger—pushing toward each other—to help the pinpoint reemerge. Push the pinpoint up through all the fabric layers. NOTE: Minimize lifting while pinning. Keep the pin and fabric as flat against the surface as possible. Check the appliqué placement with the overlay to be certain it did not shift. **FIGURE C**

4. Insert a second pin. **FIGURE D**

5. Rotate the appliqué and place a third pin. The pin faces the direction of sewing on the second side. **FIGURE E**

6. Finish pinning all around the appliqué. Use the overlay to check the final placement of the appliqué. If the piece has somehow shifted (and this does happen), reposition it now. Stitching down a perfect appliqué only to find that it's in the wrong place is definitely not a way to relax and have fun! **FIGURE F**

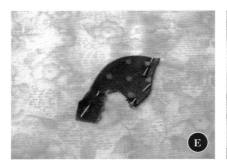

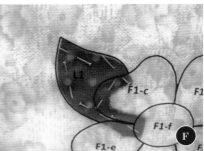

Pinning Strategies

Begin to pin-baste most appliqué shapes by inserting three stabilizing pins, distributed evenly around the perimeter. Think triangular. Additional pins (or glue) can be added between the stabilizing pins as needed.

Pin-Basting Tiny Appliqués

For tiny patches, sequin pins work best. But here's the deal: If there's room to fit at least two pins inside an appliqué, use them. However, if there's only enough room for one pin, the piece will have a tendency to pivot and will likely move while it's being stitched down. For appliqués too small for two pins, opt for glue-basting (page 51) instead. Note that even with a tiny appliqué, the pins are opposite each other in the direction that the appliqué stitches will be sewn.

Pin-Basting Large Pieces for Hand Appliqué

As pins are inserted, the appliqué and background fabric will draw in a bit. With a small appliqué, this goes unnoticed. For a larger appliqué, there will be many more pins inserted around the perimeter, so the fabric drawing in will be more noticeable. After the appliqué is stitched in place and the pins are removed, the piece and background will return to lying perfectly flat.

Here's a pinning strategy that will ensure even distribution of pins around the appliqué edge:

1. Place 2 pins a distance apart (the larger the piece, the more distant the pins).

2. Insert the next pin in the area between the 2 existing pins.

3. Repeat, filling in the blank areas at unsecured edges in increasingly smaller increments.

Glue-Basting

Glue-basting is done with water-soluble glue or basting glue. NOTE: It is recommended that the glue be washed out of the fabric at some point after the appliqué is completed.

Glue-basting is recommended for *hand appliqué* when working with motifs too small to pin-baste, for example, berries, tiny leaves, skinny stems, and bird eyes. For *machine appliqué*, glue-basting is the preferred method for temporarily securing pieces in place while they're being sewn down. For larger appliqués, inserting several pins helps to stabilize the piece before glue-basting the edges. The pins are then removed.

tip Keep the glue bottle applicator tip clean by not touching it directly with your fingers or other surfaces to minimize the risk of the contents' becoming contaminated and staining your fabric.

GATHER:

- Basting glue (Glue-Baste-It preferred)
- Pointed tool (awl, pearl-head pin, or toothpick)
- Tweezers
- Lapboard
- Background fabric
- Prepared L1 leaf appliqué
- Overlay

tip Don't glue directly over the background fabric. Glue off to the side, working on a piece of clear vinyl or scrap fabric to guard against accidentally dripping glue on your good fabric.

1. On the back side of the preturned appliqué, apply glue droplets on the seam allowances and on any raw edges around the perimeter. Glue can be applied in several ways: directly from the bottle applicator, poured in a small puddle in a dish and applied with a pointed tool, or transferred into a smaller squeeze bottle with a metal applicator tip. For hand appliqué, tiny glue drops work well. For machine appliqué, a heavier line of glue is recommended. **FIGURE A**

2. Place the appliqué on the background in the same way you would place an appliqué for pinning (page 47), but make sure the overlay is lifted enough so glue doesn't scuff onto the background. Using flat-style tweezers will help. **FIGURE B**

3. Confirm correct piece position by double-checking with the overlay, adjusting the piece as necessary. Press the piece with your fingertips to adhere.

Ready to Stitch

The appliqué is basted down, waiting to be stitched. You're all ready to settle in and make the magic happen!

Take a look at the following Gallery to gather your inspiration. If you're planning to appliqué by hand, Hand Appliqué (pages 60–82) shows you everything you need to know for simply perfect stitches. If you're going to appliqué by machine, Machine Appliqué (pages 83–91) will have you humming along in no time.

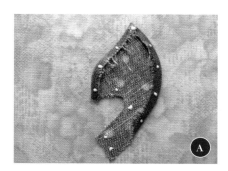

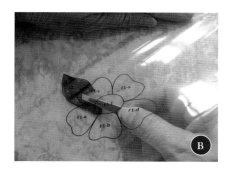

Gallery

*All gallery pieces are based on designs by Jeanne Sullivan.
Appliqué instructions, patterns, and templates are
on the accompanying CD.*

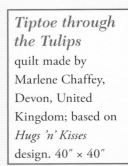

***Tiptoe through
the Tulips***
quilt made by
Marlene Chaffey,
Devon, United
Kingdom; based on
Hugs 'n' Kisses
design. 40″ × 40″

Machine appliqué, machine
quilting, bobbin embroidery,
and extensive beadwork
embellishment

Hugs 'n' Kisses
quilt made by Jean Clemens,
Williamsburg, Virginia;
designed by Jeanne Sullivan.
40″ × 40″

Hand appliqué, hand embroidery,
and hand quilting

Just for Jeanne
appliqué sampler quilt
made by Mary Cargill,
New York, New York;
based on *Just for Pretty*
design. 25″ × 25″

**Hand appliqué,
hand embroidery,
and hand quilting**

Just for Pretty
appliqué sampler quilt made by Janet Z. Esch,
Columbia, Maryland. 18″ × 18″

Hand appliqué, hand embroidery, and hand quilting

Just for Pretty
appliqué sampler quilt made by Mara Warwick,
Ankara, Turkey. 20″ × 20″

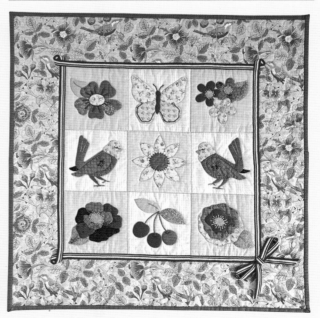

Machine appliqué, machine quilting, and hand embroidery
with border ribbon embellishment

Bird Song
made by Marlene Chaffey,
Devon, United Kingdom;
based on *Tweet Treats*
design. 12″ × 12″

Hand appliqué and
hand embroidery

Tweet Treats
made by Mary Cargill,
New York, New York.
20″ × 20″

Hand appliqué and
hand embroidery

Sunflower Glory
quilt made by Christine Maxwell
Bonney, Queensland, Australia. 34″ × 34″

Hand appliqué, hand embroidery, and hand quilting

Sunflower
made by Marlene Chaffey,
Devon, United Kingdom; based on
Sunflower Glory design. 12″ × 12″

Hand appliqué and hand embroidery

A Basketful of Hope
made by Lynn Irwin,
Sparks, Maryland.
12″ × 12″

Hand appliqué and hand embroidery

A Basketful of Hope
made by Mary Cargill,
New York, New York.
20″ × 20″

Hand appliqué and hand embroidery

Hope Sings
made by
Rosemary Clark,
Fort Myers, Florida.
21″ × 21″

**Hand appliqué,
hand embroidery,
and hand quilting**

Hope Sings quilt made by Mara Warwick,
Ankara, Turkey. 30″ × 30″

Hope Sings made by Judith Shapiro,
Riva, Maryland. 28″ × 28″

Hand appliqué, hand embroidery, and machine quilting

Machine appliqué and hand embroidery

Gallery

Hand Appliqué

Many quilters are under the impression that it takes years of practice to master the necessary skills to create fine appliqué. However, when the edges of appliqués are preturned to perfection, as you have just learned how to do, you now only need to learn a few Simply Successful Appliqué stitches to be well on your way to beautiful appliqué. Executing beautifully formed, hidden appliqué stitches is a mechanical process, quickly and easily mastered when you use the following simple, straightforward steps.

Getting Started

Choose a comfortable area to sit and stitch. Making this choice is as individual as fingerprints. I'm a comfort hound, so when stitching at home base, I seek out an upholstered chair and ottoman or a love seat with a footstool. Sometimes I prop myself up with a lot of pillows in my high poster bed. You might prefer the more structured seating offered at the kitchen table, the porch rocker, or any setup in between. But wherever you like to stitch, make certain you have good back support and the area offers bright light. Good light is helpful for many aspects of appliqué, like color planning and preparation, but bright lighting is absolutely crucial for successful stitching. Try out a lighted magnifier, too. For some, it makes a significant difference.

 tip

Stitch in Bright Light!

Even during the day, an auxiliary daylight true-color lamp will provide bright, even light and reduce eye strain. It will allow you to see tiny details with more clarity as you stitch.

Thread Selection, Preparation, and Conditioning

Selecting Thread Type and Brand

Although my first love for hand appliqué is silk thread, fine-weight cotton and machine embroidery thread are also good choices. And, in a pinch, I've been known to use a single strand of embroidery floss to get the color I needed. I find that selecting a specific thread, while important, is not as critical as sewing the actual stitches. Many thread options are available, and just about as many individual preferences, so try out all that you can.

Selecting Thread Color

For hand appliqué, choose a thread color that matches or closely blends with the color of the appliqué, not the background fabric. While nearly invisible stitches can be accomplished with widely contrasting thread (such as white on a dark-colored piece), it does take extra care to hide them, and I'd rather not worry about it. Closely matching thread to fabric is simply more forgiving.

It is important to know that thread color as it appears on the spool can be misleading. Taking time to audition a single thread stand on top of an appliqué is a fail-safe way to make thread color decisions. The goal is to find a thread that visually blends with the fabric and all but disappears when viewed at arm's length. With this approach, you'll already have a head start to making invisible stitches without having yet threaded your needle!

 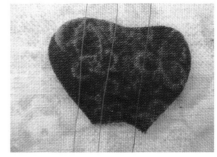

Looking at the spool colors only, you might think one of the first two would be a good match for sewing the appliqué petals; but single threads draped across the piece show the darkest red (on the right) is the closest match. In fact, it almost disappears! Without auditioning the single threads, it is doubtful that the darker spool would have been selected.

tip
When in Doubt, Go Darker

A rule of thumb is to move to a darker thread shade rather than to a lighter thread shade if you don't have a matching thread color for an appliqué.

When working with mottled or splotchy fabric containing several hues, begin by trying a thread from each color group represented in the patch and then narrow it down.

 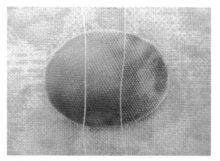

This fabric is a splotchy mix of orange, yellow, and gold. A thread in each color was auditioned initially. The gold color proved most blendable, so two golds were auditioned with the piece. The gold threads look very similar on the spool. The gold thread on the left looks lighter and brighter. The thread on the right blends better with all colors in the piece, making it a better choice.

Often, a medium gray thread is recommended as the "universal match," but in my opinion, a one-color-fits-all gray requires hard work to get it to disappear, especially on solid fabric colors. Instead, I prefer to match thread color to fabric color, reserving gray thread for multicolored prints that have quick color changes. This tricks the eye so the gray is neutralized and unnoticeable.

The gray thread draped across the purple and red solid-reading fabrics shows too much contrast, but it's barely visible on the multicolored print, making it a good choice for the multi.

Thread Preparation and Conditioning

Thread Direction

The thread that first comes off the spool is the tip end. This is the end that should be threaded into the needle's eye. Thread is spun directionally and placed on spools in a way that is intended to minimize twist while sewing.

Thread Length

A good working length for hand stitching is about 18″ (the approximate length from your middle fingertip to your elbow). Draw a length of thread from the spool, keeping track of the tip end of the thread. When using silk thread, add a few inches because it tends to be slippery and the longer doubled thread at the needle eye will allow for a better grasp.

Too long a length of sewing thread will increase the number of times the thread passes through the fabric, causing friction wear to the thread fibers. This often results in breakage, tangles, or knotting. I can't help but smile when I remember my grandmother's cautionary German saying when I'd cut a very long thread to save myself the time of frequent starts and stops: *Langes fädchen, faules mädchen!* (Long thread, lazy girl!)

Hand Appliqué **61**

Thread Conditioning

Coating thread with a thread conditioner before sewing will minimize tangling and all but eliminate backspin knots. Thread Heaven is my preference.

1. Pinch the thread at the tip end, laying it across the conditioner surface. With your left thumb, depress the thread into the conditioner while drawing the thread through it. **FIGURE A**

2. With your right hand, pull the thread up while continuing to press the thread into the conditioner, coating the entire length. **FIGURE B**

3. Holding the thread tightly at the tip end, use the left-hand fingers to stroke down the full length of the thread. Repeat 8 times (or so), continuing to stroke the thread until it feels smooth and begins to go limp.

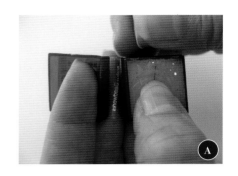

> ![] *tip* **Try This**
> *Condition two thread lengths and hold them side by side.*
> *You'll see the treated threads repel each other! So, no more knotting!*

Needle Selection and Threading

Needle Selection

Selecting an appropriate appliqué needle is of prime importance. I use Piecemakers Hand Appliqué size 12 sharps exclusively. I work a needle hard, and these needles are up to the task.

Threading an Appliqué Needle

I remember my grandmother squinting, with her needle held facing the window's light, and poking the air with her thread, trying over and over to aim straight enough to get the needle threaded. She'd often give up, mumbling in frustration. When she discovered I could thread a needle, she'd have 20 or 30 needles waiting for me to thread when I arrived for visits! I wish I could have shown her this simpler method.

By design, appliqué needles are made with a slim shaft and small eye so as not to leave noticeable holes in the fabric. Threading a small eye can be a real challenge, but not so with the following quick trick.

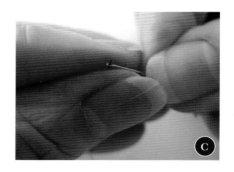

1. Cut the tip end of the thread at a slant for a fresh end with a sharp point. With your left hand, pinch the thread tip end between your thumb and index finger, leaving 1/16″ exposed. Pick up the needle by its shaft with your right hand, lowering the eye down onto the thread tip. If it's stubborn, try flipping the needle over to the other side (one side of every needle eye is shaped with a special groove to guide the thread straight into it). If that fails, then use your scissors to clip off a fresh end. Be certain to clip at an angle. Try again. **FIGURE C**

2. When the thread pops up through the needle eye, grab hold of it and pull it through.

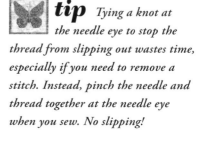

> ![] *tip* *Tying a knot at the needle eye to stop the thread from slipping out wastes time, especially if you need to remove a stitch. Instead, pinch the needle and thread together at the needle eye when you sew. No slipping!*

Knotting the Thread

Remember the spit knot? It usually came out resembling a bird's nest, but by some miracle, it managed to work. Thank goodness, someone came up with a *quilter's knot*. I use it now for making all sewing knots. It's worthwhile to take a few minutes to learn and practice it. NOTE: For silk thread, wrap the thread around the needle three times; for cotton thread, two times. This number of wraps is sufficient to anchor the thread tail without undue bulk.

The following is my version, but there are several variations.

NOTE: For appliqué, I use an appliqué needle with silk thread. Thicker perle cotton thread and a chenille needle (large scale) are used here for clearer photos.

1. Begin with a threaded needle held in your right hand. Pinch the thread tail end with your left hand, leaving an inch or so to hang free.

2. Lay the thread tail over the fingertip of your right index finger. Press down on the tail with the needle shaft held between your right thumb and middle finger. **FIGURE D**

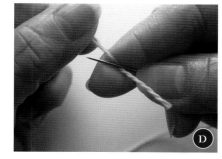

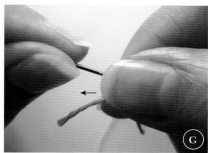

3. With your left hand, wind the thread around the needle shaft 2 or 3 times (back to front). End with the left hand in the down position, holding on to the wrapping thread. **FIGURE E**

4. Switch the thread positions: Grab the free tail end (on right), bringing it over and to the left of the wrapping thread. The wrapped thread is now tightly wound around the shaft, forming a small, tight coil on the needle. If you let go now, the thread will unwind. **FIGURE F**

5. Pinch the coil between your right thumb and index finger. No peeking! Just pinch. You'll feel the coil. Grab the point of the needle with your left hand. **FIGURE G**

6. Continue pinching the coil with your right hand while pulling leftward with your left hand as the needle and thread pass through the coil on the needle. NOTE: Twisting the needle may help the eye to pass through the coil. **FIGURE H**

7. Continue to pull leftward, drawing the entire length of thread through to the end, while still pinching the coil. It's now officially a knot. Pull the thread on both sides of the knot to tighten.

8. Clip off the thread tail, leaving ¼" beyond the knot. There you have it—a perfect knot, every time! **FIGURE I**

Finger Protection

To achieve controlled stitches, you need to feel the point of the needle on your receiving fingertip when it penetrates the fabric. I use a metal thimble for hand quilting, but feel constrained and clumsy when using one for appliqué or hand sewing. If you haven't been able to get past the awkwardness of using a thimble, a better choice is available.

When you first sit down to hand stitch, all those little needle pricks, scuffs, and scratches may go unnoticed, but it doesn't take long before they cause your fingertips to throb and sting. Hand stitching doesn't have to be painful! Thimble-It is a package of small, oval-shaped, clear plastic sticky pads that come on peel-off sheets. Placing a pad on sensitive spots will allow you to stitch all day without having your fingers get sore. The best part is that you can still feel the needle point as if your fingertips weren't covered.

Everyone holds the needle and feels for the point in a slightly different way, and sometimes with alternate fingers. As you begin to sew, pay close attention to where the needle pricks are landing and where the needle's eye is indenting your pushing finger. Apply a pad to each of these areas and you'll never get to the stage where you need to stop sewing because it's too hurtful or you're leaving a blood trail on your work! If a Thimble-It pad is too big, cut it to a size that is more comfortable.

Controlling Background Fabric Bulk

The background fabric for an appliqué design can be any size or shape. When sewing on a small background, the appliqués are easy to reach and your hand is comfortable while you stitch. As the size of the background increases, the amount of fabric bulk increases, making it more difficult to reach the appliqués in the center of the block. To control excess fabric, fold over the edges once, twice, or more to minimize the reach and grasp the edges comfortably. NOTE: As you appliqué around the perimeter of a piece, the folds can be unfolded and refolded often to allow for the best hand position.

Hand Positioning for Appliqué

Holding the Fabric

Positioning your hands properly to hold the fabric and your sewing needle accomplishes two important things: First, your hands will remain in a natural position without strain, allowing you to stitch longer and more comfortably. Second, you're all set up for making beautiful, invisible appliqué stitches!

Note that the fingers work in pairs: The index and middle fingers extend to hold the top edge of the background fabric and appliqué. The thumb and ring finger work together to hold and manipulate the area of the appliqué that will be stitched. The pinkie can rest underneath where it's comfortable. The wrist is straight, not bent. After you get the idea, you'll naturally grab onto the fabric in one motion.

Holding the Needle

The hand should pull the thread vertically, in a straight-up trajectory, or slightly angled to the right. The hand is relaxed, with all fingers helping. The wrist is not bent.

Caution! Though tempting, *do not use* the ring finger or pinkie on your sewing hand by extending it to help direct the thread as it is drawn upward. Over time, this places undue strain on tendons.

 tip *Get into the habit of holding the needle at the eye where the thread is doubled. This will prevent the thread from slipping out of the eye, interrupting your sewing as you rethread the needle.*

Invisible Appliqué Stitches

Appliqué stitches are used to sew the piece to the background fabric. The goal is to execute an invisible stitch. Hand appliqué requires patience and consistency more so than it does fine sewing skills. You'll be happy to know that appliqué stitches are technically very simple and easily mastered.

Simply Successful Appliqué uses a different approach to stitching than other appliqué methods. Because the stitches begin slightly *in* from the edge and emerge exactly *on* the edge, they are truly invisible. The stitches on the back are perpendicular to or slanted toward the line of stitching, not parallel to the line as in traditional appliqué.

Simply Successful Appliqué comprises three different stitches, each with a specific purpose: the appliqué stab stitch, the appliqué surface stitch, and the appliqué wrapping stitch. Learning these mainstay appliqué stitches will allow you to use each one to its best advantage.

note *For visual clarity, the step-by-step instructions are presented using photo sequences featuring a large chenille sewing needle, heavy perle cotton thread, and thick wool fabric with high color contrast.*

Simply Successful Appliqué Stab Stitch

A stab stitch is the easiest stitch to make and the most versatile. In fact, you really only need to learn this one stitch to be able to sew on every one of your preturned appliqués for any project. To execute the stab stitch, your sewing hand will alternate between sewing above the background fabric and sewing beneath it. It is a two-step stitch.

The blue wool represents the background fabric, and the black wool represents a straight-edge appliqué patch with a preturned edge. The black appliqué piece is pin-basted onto the blue background fabric.

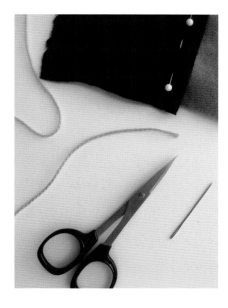

GATHER:
- Preturned and basted appliqué
- Cut length of thread
- Needle
- Scissors

1. Begin by threading a needle and tying a quilter's knot (page 63). With your left hand, pick up the appliqué using proper hand positioning (page 64). Pick up the threaded needle in your right hand. **FIGURE A**

 tip
Knot Notes

Intentionally, I do not begin stitching at the front of the work by burying the knot between the appliqué and its preturned seam allowance. I don't want the knot to shadow up through the piece and be seen on the appliqué surface, especially when I am working with lighter fabric colors. Knots in the seam allowance can also cause a lump in the surface of an appliqué. I place my knots at the back of the work, toward the inside edge of the appliqué, so they remain hidden. Any knot lump will nestle into the batting at the back of the work when the piece is quilted.

2. Bring the needle straight up from beneath the background, stabbing the point up through all fabric layers, emerging a short distance to the left of the turned edge. If the needle does not peek out where you want it, simply pull down from underneath and try to stab it up again. It may take a few pokes to get it right. Within a short time, your judgment will be refined and you'll get it on the first attempt. Keep in mind that it doesn't have to be exact—it's just a probing poke to get you in the range: not too near the folded edge and not too deep inside the appliqué. **FIGURE B**

3. Once you're satisfied with the location of your up stab, begin to slowly pull back the needle until the point drops *below* the surface of the appliqué (between the underside of the piece and the turned-edge seam allowance). If you draw back too much and the point comes out below the background fabric, just poke it back up to the surface and try again.

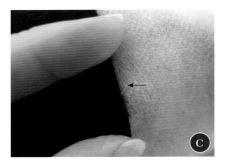

4. Tilt the needle to the right (feeling the point scrape along the appliqué underside) and stab the point out *exactly* at the crease in the folded edge. If necessary, try again to get it right by withdrawing and restabbing the needle point. When the needle point is poking out through the edge fold, push the needle from underneath, extending it onto the surface. **FIGURE C**

5. Release your grip on the needle and bring your sewing hand to the top of the work. Grab the needle, pulling up the entire length of thread to the surface. The knot will grab from underneath to anchor this first stab stitch. Give the thread a gentle tug so the knot is snug underneath the background. **FIGURE D**

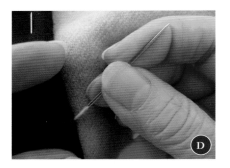

6. Direct the thread to the left to rest on the appliqué, and hold the thread out of the way with your left thumb. **FIGURE E**

7. With your sewing hand, stab the needle straight down into the background fabric next to the previous stitch that emerged from the fold. The needle shaft should barely brush against the appliqué edge. **FIGURE F**

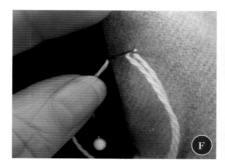

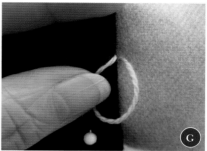

8. Move your sewing hand underneath the background again, pulling the needle and thread through to the back of the work. Keeping your surface thumb on the thread will help to form an even loop and minimize thread twist as the thread is drawn to the back. Continue to pull the thread from underneath, lifting your thumb to free the loop when it becomes small. **FIGURE G**

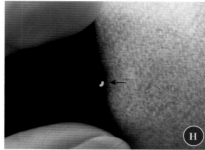

9. Give the thread a little tug, pulling it gently but firmly, to keep the thread snug as it nestles in to hold down the edge of the appliqué. Notice how the stitch is barely visible even though the thread is thick and a contrasting color. **FIGURE H**

tip *For invisible stab stitches, tilting the work so you can see straight down on it (from a bird's-eye view) will help you to place the down stitch precisely next to where the up stitch emerged. Avoid a down stitch placed at a slant (either forward or behind the up stitch). Slanted stitches are **not** invisible.*

10. Repeat the stab stitch sequence (up/down), continuing around the perimeter of the appliqué. NOTE: By making appliqué stitches in this way, you are taking small hidden sideways bites through both the background *and* the turned-under seam allowance.

Simply Successful Appliqué Surface Stitch

A surface appliqué stitch is a good choice for stitching broader shapes because each stitch can be taken in one step for a rhythmic, faster stitching cycle. The needle, thread, and sewing hand remain on the surface of the background fabric, which reduces the time it takes to make each stitch. When compared with stab stitches, surface stitches appear identical on the front of the work, even to the discerning eye.

If surface stitches take half the time and look the same, why not use them all the time? Because of the wider area needed to manipulate the needle—the shape of the appliqué piece may be too narrow or change too quickly to make the surface stitches close enough to hold down the edges adequately. It would be like trying to make a U-turn with your car in a narrow driveway. Surface stitches are used mainly for appliqués with straight edges or gentle slopes and contours.

1. Begin with a thread emerging from an edge fold, holding it down (to the left) with your thumb. For greater control, position your sewing hand with palm facing up. Hold the needle between the thumb and index finger (with the shaft resting on the index tip and thumb pulled back slightly). The needle point should protrude out front, making it easy to see where to insert it: straight down, next to where the thread is coming out of the fold crease. **FIGURE I**

2. Aim the needle point toward the left, making a down-and-up scooping motion, taking a bite of the background fabric and bringing up the needle point to the surface, just to the left of the folded appliqué edge. **FIGURE J**

3. Tilt back both hands as you make the stitch so that the edge of the appliqué rises and forms a ridge with the fold facing up. Draw back the needle point to recede just below the surface of the appliqué fabric. **FIGURE K**

4. Poke the needle point up through the fold crease. **FIGURE L**

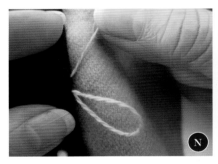

5. Begin to pull the needle and thread to the surface. **FIGURE M**

6. Nearing the end of the thread length, tuck the needle between your ring finger and palm, freeing up your index finger and thumb. Then, pinch and pull the thread as a stitch loop begins to form. The stitch is better controlled this way. **FIGURE N**

7. Pull the thread up until the stitch nestles into the fold and the edge hugs the surface of the background fabric. **FIGURE O**

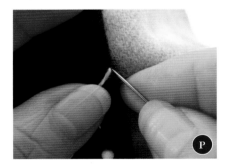

8. To repeat the sequence for the next surface appliqué stitch, begin by moving the thread to the left, holding it down with your thumb. Continue along the length of the seam or until a curvy profile requires you to transition to stab stitches. **FIGURE P**

Simply Successful Appliqué Wrapping Stitch

Wrapping stitches serve to reinforce the weave structure of fabric when it is necessary to clip inside a deep curve or a deep V of a preturned appliqué piece. Wrapping stitches will prevent vulnerable areas from fraying.

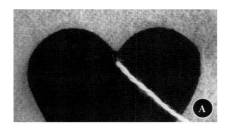

Appliqué wrapping stitches come in two versions. One you already know. These are simply appliqué stab stitches (pages 65–67) made closely together, side by side. Executed in fragile areas, they work to anchor the patch to the background while stabilizing the clipped areas. These stitches are invisible.

The second way to make appliqué wrapping stitches is usually only necessary for the deepest inside V. Sometimes, no matter how much sizing is used or how much care is taken when removing the template, a fabric edge may unravel near the clip. In this case, wrapping stitches (made like embroidery satin stitches) will stabilize and hold the vulnerable area secure while also preventing fray. Wrapping stitches do *not* poke through the fold crease but rather come up through the surface two or three woven threads inside the appliqué edge and reenter the background as usual (next to the folded edge). These side-by-side stitches are *not* invisible. They are seen on the surface of the piece as they wrap around the turned edges, so it is necessary for the thread color to *match the appliqué color* as closely as possible.

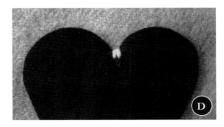

1. Appliqué wrapping stitch (second type): Bring the thread up to the inside of the V. **FIGURE A**

2. Complete the wrapping stitch with a stab stitch taken straight down into the background, next to the appliqué edge. **FIGURE B**

3. Bring the thread up to the right, beside the first wrapping stitch. **FIGURE C**

4. Complete the second wrapping stitch with a stab stitch down, beside the first stitch. **FIGURE D**

5. Bring the thread up to the left, next to the center wrapping stitch. **FIGURE E**

6. Complete the third wrapping stitch with a down stab stitch. **FIGURE F**

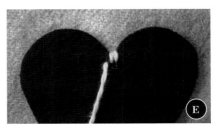

Additional wrapping stitches can be placed to the left and right of a clipped inside V or a deep inside curve, as needed, to secure all frayed or fragile edge areas. NOTE: When executing wrapping stitches using silk or fine cotton thread, there is more room for adding stitches without the bulk, if needed.

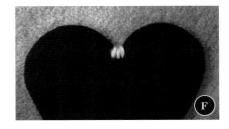

This appliqué heart has seven wrapping stitches securing the fragile area inside the deep V: a center stitch with three stitches on each side of the center. Silk thread causes no bulky thread buildup, and using a matching thread color ensures the stitches will be barely noticeable (even when viewed close up).

tip *Try to coax a stubborn, frayed fabric thread into place using a wooden toothpick. For clipped V threads that simply will not behave, apply a dot of Liquid Stitch, a permanent fabric glue, to the woven threads on the back of the V with a pinpoint. Stitch as usual.*

Tack Stitch for Appliqué

A tack stitch is essentially an up–down stitch, which can be used to attach dimensional elements. A tack stitch is taken from beneath the background layer, up through the top of the appliqué (taking a bite of the motif), and then returning through all layers to the back side of the work. When the thread is pulled taut, it grabs the appliqué element with a tiny loop stitch. Use tack stitches to attach a puff blossom with tiny stitches taken on the underside of the petals around the perimeter. For a stuffed berry, make the tack stitches in a small area clustered on the berry bottom, keeping all stitches neatly hidden.

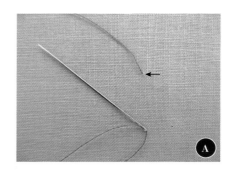

Another use of the tack stitch is for ruching (pages 102–104). After the fabric is drawn up in gathers, the ruched arrangement is secured by distributing a series of hidden tack stitches within the folds. The tack stitches can be placed apart from one another, with the thread traveling on the underside of the work.

Tack stitches must be tensioned evenly—snug enough to anchor the element, but without causing the background fabric to pucker.

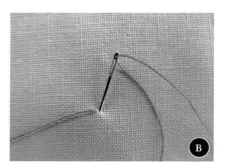

The following shows how to make tack stitches, keeping in mind that actual tack stitches are hidden:

1. Bring the needle and thread up to the surface of the fabric from beneath the background. **FIGURE A**

2. Insert the needle down, next to the emerging thread (but *not* sharing the same hole). **FIGURE B**

3. Pull the needle and thread through to the back of the work to complete the tack stitch. **FIGURE C**

Stitch Tension

Being mindful of stitch tension is another important consideration for hand appliqué. How tightly you snug up the thread can affect the appearance of the finished work considerably. If you pull too tight on the thread as it draws the appliqué against the background, the appliqué can have a puckered look. If your thread tension is too loose, the edges will not be secure, the stitches will show from the front, and the appliqués can shift out of place.

To get a good sense of the correct thread tension, turn your piece over to the wrong side of the work and try the following tension test. (A heavyweight cotton thread is used for the illustrations so that the stitches will show up well.)

Using the eye end of an appliqué needle, scoop beneath a stitch and gently lift it. If the thread lifts easily, raising a loop, the thread tension is much too loose.

If the stitch can't be lifted easily because it's hugging the background fabric, the stitch is properly tensioned.

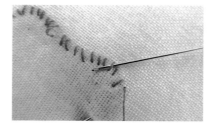

During hand appliquéing, a gentle tug on the thread at the end of each stitch will help the piece snug up against the background. By knowing how to test your stitch tension, you'll be able to refine how you take that tug.

Stitch Gauge

The number of stitches needed to adequately hold down an appliqué edge depends in part upon the weight and type of fabric. When working with quilter's cottons, it's my opinion that any stitches more than ⅛″ apart are "toe snaggers" (too far apart). Try to make stitches no more than ⅛″ apart when you first learn to appliqué, even if you have to stick with stab stitches for a while as you're working to learn the surface stitches. Set a goal for yourself of ¹⁄₁₆″ apart, or 16 stitches per inch. When you get comfortable, your fine motor skills and hand–eye coordination will kick in to refine your movements and you'll end up automatically making smaller stitches. In fact, it will actually become difficult for you to sew larger stitches after you learn to execute the smaller ones.

With 16 stitches or more per inch, you'll be making the appliqué one with the background fabric. The pieces will be secure with no chance of their edges lifting or fraying. And,

happily, there will be no puckering around the appliqué edges when the piece is quilted or washed.

Stitches per inch:	1″	Rating:
7 or fewer	I I I I I I	Toe snaggers (too far apart)
8	I I I I I I I I	Not quite there
12	IIIIIIIIIIII	Good
16	IIIIIIIIIIIIIIII	Goal
20	IIIIIIIIIIIIIIIIIIII	Best
24	IIIIIIIIIIIIIIIIIIIIIIII	For tiny shapes

 tip
Unstitching

When you've made a stitch that you're not happy with, stop and take it out immediately. If it's bothering you now, it will continue to haunt you. It's much faster and easier to remove it before you sew in nine more stitches and then decide it has to come out.

Basting Down Raw Edges

A running stitch or running backstitch is recommended to secure any raw edges on preturned appliqués. This step prevents the cut edges from fraying or catching the thread while you work on other pieces. Most importantly, basting down raw edges will prevent them from shifting as you pin or sew on the next appliqué layer, which will cover the raw edge.

A running stitch and running backstitch can be sewn using up-and-down stab stitches (two-steps) but are more quickly executed as surface stitches. They have a job to do, but they don't need to be particularly neat since they'll be covered by the next appliqué layer. Sew these stitches within the seam allowance.

Baste raw edges.

Running Stitch

A running stitch is a series of stitches made by inserting the needle point in and out of the fabric at even intervals. Because running stitches are executed on the surface, several stitches can be collected onto the needle shaft before drawing the needle and thread through the fabric. Reserve running stitches for basting down small areas of raw edges.

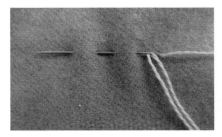

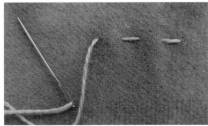

Running Backstitch Combination

To secure larger areas of raw edges on an appliqué, use what I call a *running backstitch*. It's a combination stitch, used to hold the fabric layers more securely than a basic running stitch. Also executed on the surface, the running backstitch consists of a running stitch followed by a scooped backstitch.

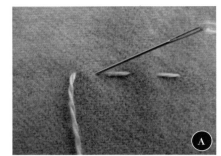
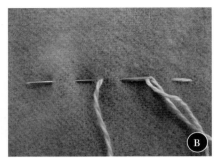

1. The running backstitch begins with 2 running stitches. Next, take a backstitch by inserting the needle point between the emerging thread and the previous stitch. **FIGURE A**

2. Complete the backstitch by bringing the needle point up, followed by another running stitch. **FIGURE B**

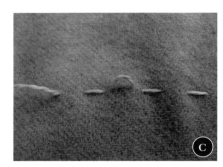

3. Pull the thread and needle through the fabric. A backstitch loop will form just prior to pulling the thread completely through. **FIGURE C**

Controlling Thread Twist

When stitching by hand, whether to sew on a button, mend a hem, or appliqué, most times you'll notice that the sewing thread begins to twist. The problem with thread twist is that as it builds up, it can cause a backspin twist knot, which is nearly impossible to untie.

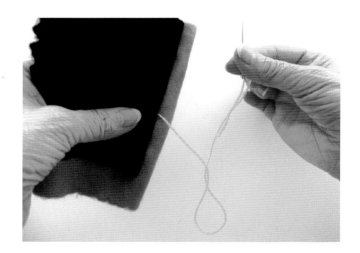

Luckily, there's an easy remedy for twist: Untwist it! Untwisting is done by twirling the needle to the right for right-handers or to the left for lefties. When you notice the thread twisting, usually one or two needle twirls will do, but don't overdo it or you'll get a twist going in the opposite direction.

Surface stitches have a tendency to twist the thread more than stab stitches. For either stitch, you'll need to untwist more frequently as the sewing thread gets shorter.

 tip
Anticipate Twist and Avoid Knots
The best way to deal with twist knots is to avoid them altogether. Keep an eye on the loop formed after a stitch is taken and the thread length is drawn up. It's safe to proceed if the loop is well formed and tightens without distorting.

Well-formed loop, no thread twist, no danger of knots

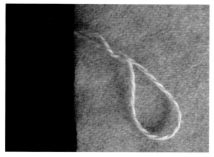

Twisted loop: Pull thread through slowly, allowing it to unwind as it passes through fabric; untwist thread (page 72) before next stitch.

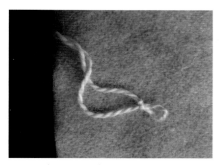

Too much twist can backspin and knot. If you can't untie it, clip off the knot, unstitch enough stitches to regain a thread tail, pull the tail through to the back side, thread it back onto the needle, and tie off. With a new thread, begin again where you left off.

 **tip** *Checking for thread twist will become intuitive and automatic as you sew.*

Tying Off Threads

Tying off, also known as ending off or knotting a thread end, is executed at the back of the work. Small backstitches can be sewn into the back side of the background fabric behind the appliqué without showing up on the front side of the work.

Tying off well is essential to making stitches stay put and not loosen over time. When done properly, the thread tail is triple-knotted and then buried between the layers of the background fabric and the appliqué.

1. After an appliqué piece is stitched, bring the thread to the back of the work. Take a small backstitch into the background fabric only. Bring the needle point up in the same place as the emerging thread. Push up the needle fully, and grasp it with your sewing hand. **FIGURE D**

2. Pull the emerging thread toward the left until a loop begins to form. Insert the needle upward through the loop, drawing the thread away from you. **FIGURE E**

3. Continue to draw the thread up through to the end. Tug on the thread to tighten the loop, forming a knot. Take a scooping backstitch, beginning at the base of the knot and reemerging a little beyond the first knot. Pull the needle through and toward the left. **FIGURE F**

4. Tug the thread to pull the loop closed, reinforcing the *second* knot. **FIGURE G**

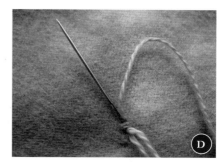

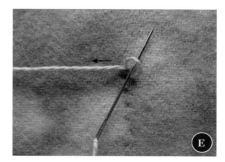

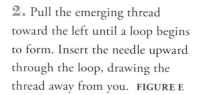

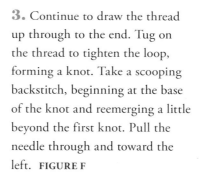

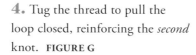

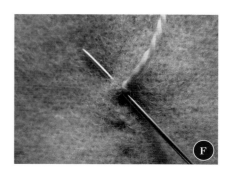

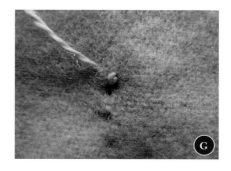

5. With the needle facing toward you, insert the point at the top of the knot, reemerging below the knot between the background fabric and the appliqué—this forms the *third* knot. **FIGURE H**

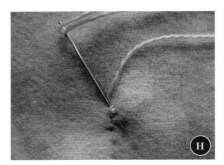

6. Tug the thread to tighten the loop. The tail emerges to the right of the stitches (behind the appliqué shape). **FIGURE I**

7. Clip thread close to the surface where the tail emerges. The triple knot is complete. **FIGURE J**

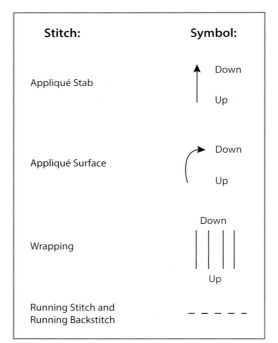

 tip
New Piece, New Thread
When you start a new appliqué piece, there might be enough thread remaining on your needle to sew on another piece, but it's likely to have worn thin or become subtly frayed. It's safer to discard this excess thread and rethread your needle with a fresh length.

Appliqué Stitch Maps and Symbols

A stitch map will help you to know which stitches to use as you sew around a preturned appliqué piece. Stitch symbols (representing each type of appliqué stitch) will enable you to read an appliqué stitch map. There are no hard-and-fast rules. These are only suggestions, a way for you to feel comfortable. Work the way that is easiest and most satisfying for you. Refer back to these stitch maps as needed for the appliqué shapes you are working with.

Appliqué Stitch Maps

Stitch maps show stitch type and direction; they are not to scale/size or to gauge/number of stitches.

Simply Successful Appliqué Stitch Symbols

Stitch:	Symbol:
Appliqué Stab	↑ Down / Up
Appliqué Surface	↱ Down / Up
Wrapping	Down |||| Up
Running Stitch and Running Backstitch	– – – – –

Hand Appliqué Tutorials for Common Shapes and Contours

Below you'll find stitch maps and detailed photos to help you complete the petals and flower center for the F1 flower. You'll also find stitch maps for other common appliqué shapes and contours. After you've sewn down a few appliqués, you'll be off and running on your own.

Important: On the CD, you'll find detailed photo tutorials for Start to Finish: Hand Stitching an Appliqué Flower (pages CD1–CD4).

Leaf

Below is the stitching sequence used to appliqué a leaf.

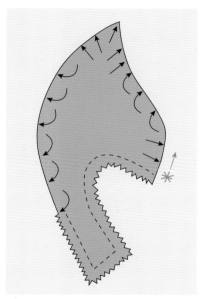

Leaf stitch map

Reading the leaf stitch map: The green asterisk and arrow indicate the starting spot and direction of stitching. Begin with two or three stab stitches. Switch to surface stitches on the curved side of the piece. Switch back to stab stitches for the leaf tip. Go back to surface stitches when you reach the second curved side of the leaf. Secure the bottom raw edges with running stitches. Bring the thread to the back and tie off.

Flower Petal

Below is the stitching sequence used to appliqué a petal. All five petals in the F1 flower are similar, so you'll get a lot of practice. Complete them in alphabetical order: F1-a, F1-b, F1-c, F1-d, and F1-e.

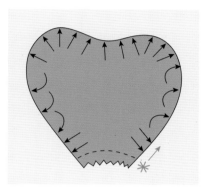

Petal stitch map

Reading the petal stitch map: The green asterisk and arrow indicate the starting spot and direction of stitching. Begin with two or three stab stitches. Switch to surface stitches on the curved side of the patch. When the curve becomes too narrow for easy surface stitches, switch back to stab stitches for the wavy curves along the top petal edge. Go back to surface stitches when you reach the second side of the petal. End with a few stab stitches as you near the raw edge. Secure the bottom raw edge with running stitches. Bring the thread to the back and tie off.

 tip *You might find it easier to use stab stitches when you stitch the part of the petal layered onto the leaf.*

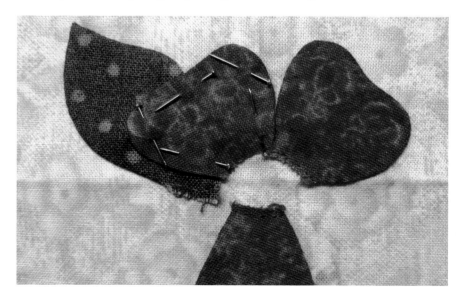

Flower Center

The center of the F1 flower is an oval shape. The tight curve around a small oval or circle doesn't allow for easy manipulation of the needle for closely placed surface stitches. Also, you are now adding another appliqué layer on top of the petal layer, so stab stitches are a good choice for the entire piece. Remember to end a stitch or two past the first stitch. Bring thread to back and tie off.

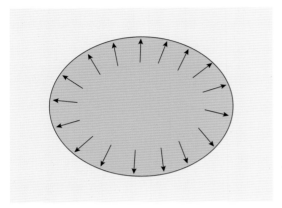

Oval stitch map

Straight Edge

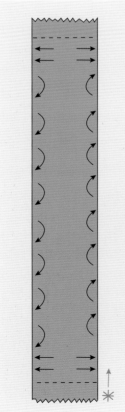

Straight-edge stitch map

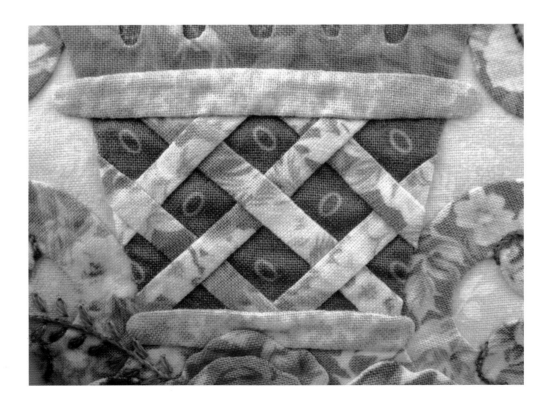

Curves

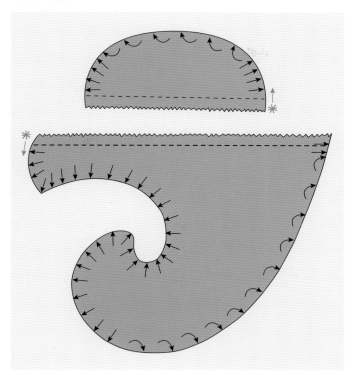

Curve stitch maps

Circle

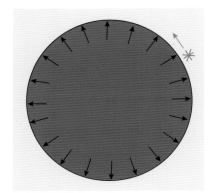

Circle stitch map

Wavy Curves

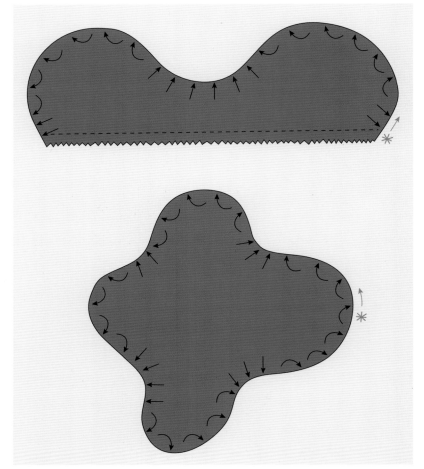

Outside and inside curves stitch maps

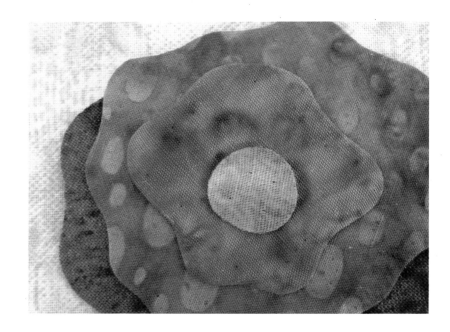

Inside U

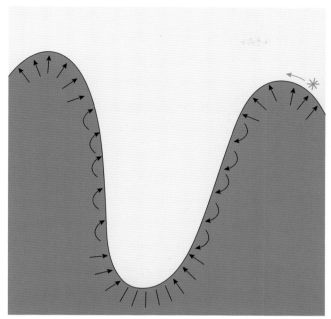

Inside U stitch map

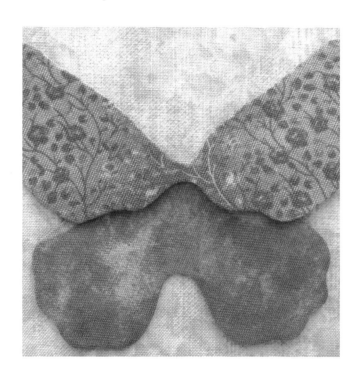

Inside V

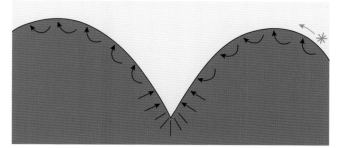

Inside V stitch map

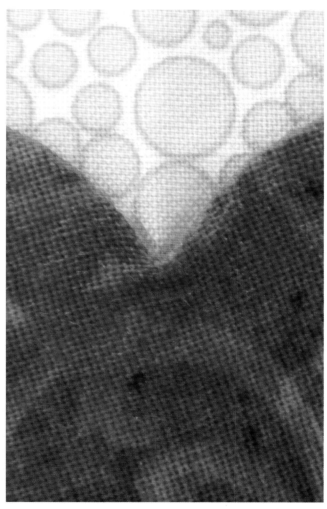

On the Point

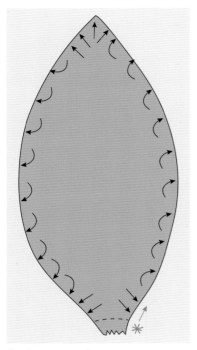

On-the-point stitch map

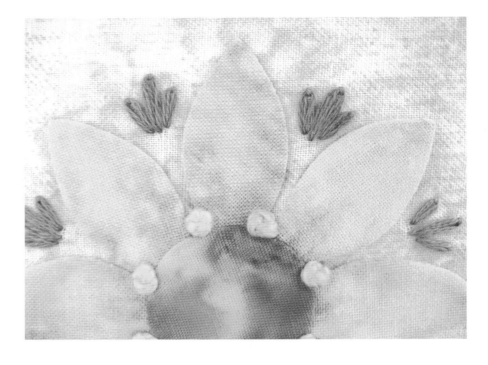

Reverse Appliqué

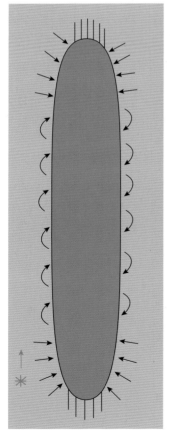

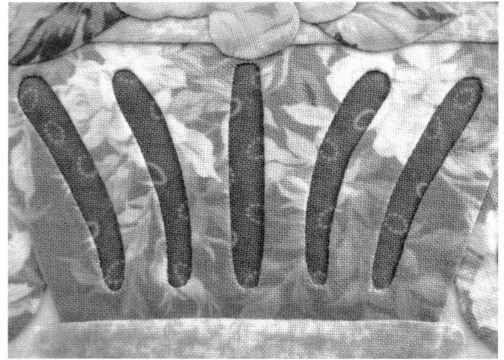

For reverse appliqué, the fabric layer showing up through the appliqué is treated as the background fabric. Hand stitching for reverse appliqué is executed clockwise around the inside perimeter for right-handers, counterclockwise for lefties.

Reverse appliqué stitch map

General Guidelines for Hand Appliqué Stitch Selection

- Begin sewing with two or three *stab stitches*. This will draw up the knot to the back of the work and anchor the beginning turned edge of the appliqué.

- Use *surface stitches* where possible and comfortable for single-layer areas of the appliqué. Surface stitches work well for straight lines and gentle curves.

- Use *stab stitches* for areas where pieces will overlap in layers. Stab stitches can handle the bulk of layered fabric while creating a smooth appliqué seam. Stab stitches are also effective for tight curves, small circles, and amoeba-like shapes with a lot of wavy contours.

- Use *wrapping stab stitches* for vulnerable inside V shapes such as the inside V of a heart shape. Placing several side-by-side wrapping stitches at the clip will reinforce the weave structure.

- Anchor all raw edges with *running stitches* or *running backstitches* to stabilize the area where another piece will overlap them. Anchoring raw edges will prevent the pieces from shifting.

- For closed appliqués (as in a circle or ring shape) the stitching begins and ends at the same place. Take one or two stitches beyond the first stitch before bringing the thread to the back of the work to tie off.

Working in Layers

Pieces can be stitched on top of each other for layered appliqué using either stab stitches or surface stitches (just as for single-layer appliqué). There are some differences, however, in the execution of the stitches and the way the pieces will appear when the appliqué is finished. Using stab stitches exclusively will make it easier to penetrate all the layers of fabric as they build up. There will also be a slight depression along the patch edges, creating a subtle dimensional effect. Surface stitching can be used for layered appliqué, too, manipulating the background to take bites of fabric by skimming the surface of the pieces in the previous layers.

Multilayered appliqué penny rose from *A Basketful of Hope* (page 124)

Off-Block Construction

Rather than placing and sewing your pieces on the background one at a time, another option for hand appliqué is preassembling: Preassemble a motif by glue-basting the individual patches together into one unit. Next, apply basting glue to the unit perimeter and glue-baste the unit onto the background fabric where overlapping seams and the perimeter are stitched. Alternatively, the glue-basted motif can be stitched off-block and then glue-basted to the background, where it is appliquéd around the perimeter.

This technique works especially well for managing small flowers with a lot of pieces or when working on very large projects, minimizing the number of times you need to use the overlay for placement.

Flower motifs have been preassembled (off-block) by gluing and stitching before being appliquéd as a whole unit onto the background fabric (preassembled motifs made by Robbyn Robinson).

You now have all the skills you need to do hand appliqué, from simple, small projects to intricate Baltimore Album quilts. Even the most intricate designs are made up of the same basic, common appliqué shapes, lines, and contours. Any differences simply boil down to the number and size of the pieces.

You are now ready to move on to Special Appliqué Techniques (pages 97–118) and then to Projects (pages 121–125) for a peek at the project photos. Complete project instructions, master patterns, and template patterns are on the CD.

Machine Appliqué

Even a diehard hand appliquér (like me) enjoys making machine stitched projects every now and then. The Simply Successful Appliqué turned-edge technique is the perfect solution for getting the look of hand stitching without sewing it by hand. But the best part is you'll be thoroughly delighted that your machine appliqué can stand up to the closest scrutiny and be accomplished in less time than sewing by hand. If you can thread a sewing machine, you can machine appliqué.

Springtime's Promise quilt made by Mara Warwick, Ankara, Turkey. Machine appliqué, machine embroidery, and machine quilting. 30″ (diameter) octagonal quilt.

note *Please take the time to read through the entire chapter to get the total picture. Trust me on this one! When you're done reading the pictures and text, you'll be able to dive right in.*

Sewing Machine Features

A basic sewing machine capable of making zigzag stitches will do the job. Having a *needle-down* option will make life a little easier, but it's not essential. The needle-down function automatically sets the machine to end with the needle point down in the fabric when you take your foot off the foot control to stop. Otherwise, simply stop the machine and sink the needle manually by turning the hand wheel when you need to. With the needle down, you can raise the presser foot to pivot the piece in position as you line up the next stitch. The presser foot is then lowered to hold the appliqué tightly against the feed dogs before continuing to stitch.

Choosing a Presser Foot

Use an open-toe presser foot. The open toe allows you to visually track the folded edge so you can easily control where the stitches will land.

Let's make it easy for you. Here's my choice and why:

If you have a Bernina, it's the #37 Patchwork Foot. If you don't have a Bernina, use a foot that looks like this one. It has two ideal attributes for Simply Successful machine appliqué techniques:

- It keeps the fabric layers pressed firmly against the feed dogs for even stitching.

- The graduated open toe has a wider open area at the front of the foot and a narrower needle/stitch zone for more accurate stitch placement.

Thread Selection

For machine appliqué, I recommend two specific combinations of upper thread and bobbin thread to create even zigzag stitches with consistent results. Either combination creates a nearly invisible top stitch, while the bobbin stitch forms a soft and subtle padding beneath.

- Sulky monofilament with Mettler cotton 50-weight
- Superior MonoPoly with Mettler cotton 50-weight

Or, try experimenting with another cotton 50-weight thread.

Top (Upper) Thread

Use Sulky Invisible 100% polyester monofilament or Superior MonoPoly polyester thread. Polyester is superfine and doesn't seem to catch the light like its nylon counterpart, so stitches are less noticeable. It remains soft and flexible and washes well. It does not melt with normal ironing (up through a cotton setting). It does not yellow over time. Placed on a vertical spool pin, it will not unravel.

Use clear for light- to medium-colored appliqués and smoke for dark-colored appliqués.

Bobbin Thread

Select a bobbin thread color to match the background fabric. Fill the bobbin three-fourths full. The 50-weight thread will help to keep the bobbin stitch below the fabric surface.

Needle Selection

Fine-diameter upper sewing thread calls for a corresponding size fine machine needle. Schmetz brand Microtex sharp needles in size 60/8 offer a very thin shaft and an especially fine, sharp point for even stitches. These needles pair up perfectly with monofilament thread, making the holes in the fabric barely noticeable. More importantly, tiny needle holes help to discourage the bobbin thread loops from popping up to the surface.

Preventing Thread Nests

Avoid the risk of thread nests by *always* bringing the bobbin thread to the top of the stitch plate each time you're ready to start sewing.

Caution: Whenever you need to draw thread out from the needle, raise the foot to disengage the tension disks and coax it through the machine thread path by moving the hand wheel forward and back to loosen it, keeping an eye on the flexing needle. Pulling too hard can break the thread or snap the needle!

Pulling Up Bobbin Tail after Inserting Fabric

To ensure your bobbin tail won't get jammed up underneath, insert your fabric first, lining up your needle starting place on the appliqué edge (appliqué is not shown for detail clarity). Lower the presser foot, manually turn the hand wheel far forward to sink the needle deep into the fabric, and then turn it way back to bring up a bobbin thread loop to the surface while also pulling on the monofilament upper thread. Pull up the loop until the bobbin tail emerges on the surface. Hold on to the thread tails when you start sewing.

Machine Stitch and Tension Settings

There's no universal, one-size-fits-all rule for stitch and tension settings, so you'll need to adjust the settings to suit your particular machine. The good news is that you'll only need to figure it out once. Start with the settings below; then prepare a few sample preturned appliqué pieces to give your stitches and settings a test run.

Settings to Get You Started

When using the special combination of very fine monofilament with regular-weight cotton thread, you'll need to adjust the machine tensions to balance the stitches properly. The following settings should get you close; then adjust as needed. They are a good starting place because the stitches are not too narrow and they're close enough in length for you to be in control as you navigate most curves.

Stitch width   Start with a zigzag stitch width set to 1.0.

Stitch length   Start with a zigzag stitch length set to 1.5.

Upper stitch tension   Start with the top tension set to between 1 and 2 points lower than normal.

Bobbin stitch tension   For a Bernina, insert the bobbin thread through the bobbin case finger for increased lower thread tension. For other machines, see your owner's manual. Typically, you can increase tension by turning the bobbin case screw to the right. Try this in small increments, testing after each change.

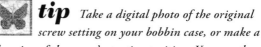 **tip**   *Take a digital photo of the original screw setting on your bobbin case, or make a drawing of the screw's starting position. You can then easily and accurately reset it to the default setting when you want to return to normal sewing work.*

Later, when you're feeling more comfortable, try varying the adjustments as you make samples, using a narrower stitch width (goal: 0.8 or 0.9 width setting) while adjusting the length to fit the profile of the patch.

- The smaller the piece or the tighter the curves, the shorter the length, as short as 1.3.

- The broader the profile, the longer the stitch, up to 1.8 length.

- A longer zigzag stitch reduces thread tension on the appliqué edge, creating a smoother profile with less noticeable stitches.

- The narrower the zigzag stitch (while you're still able to stay in control), the closer the stitches can be to the edge of the appliqué, making needle holes less noticeable.

Appliqué Zigzag Stitching

For quality machine stitching, it's a good idea to work out some of the sewing techniques on preturned sample appliqué pieces. You'll be happy for the chance to become better acquainted with how your machine handles and get to know what to expect from your needle, thread, and appliqués.

 tip
Zig and Zag

- Zig—*the stitch made with the needle down in the background fabric*

- Zag—*the stitch made with the needle down in the edge of the appliqué*

1. Prepare and stabilize the background fabric with stiff sizing (pages 13–16).

2. When glue-basting for machine appliqué, apply a thin continuous line of water-soluble basting glue to all preturned appliqué edges as well as any raw cut edges. Basting glue (applied a bit more heavily than for hand stitching) will hold the piece in place on the background fabric and provide a stiff edge to machine appliqué. When working with larger pieces, use a few pins to anchor the appliqué temporarily while lifting the edges, gluing a section at a time. Afterward, all glue will be removed when the completed project is washed. **FIGURE A**

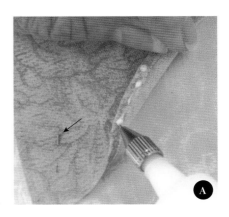

3. Press the glued edges with your fingertips as you go, ensuring adhesion to background fabric. Check that all the edges are held securely before stitching.

4. Manually turn the machine hand wheel until the needle begins to move to the *right* side of the zigzag stitching cycle (in readiness for taking a *zig* stitch).

5. For open appliqués, orient the piece to begin stitching next to a raw edge. Right-handers should plan to stitch clockwise around the shape; lefties, counterclockwise.

6. Lift the presser foot. Slide the background fabric between the stitch plate and raised presser foot, lining up the appliqué at the starting point. Bring up the bobbin thread and hold both threads to the left, moving the piece toward the needle area. Turn the hand wheel to sink the needle point precisely into the background fabric, to the right side of the edge fold. (Threads not shown.) **FIGURE B**

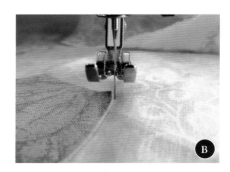

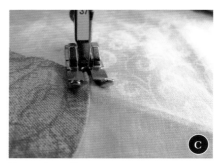

Zig stitch needle position

> *tip* When stitching begins, the threads will be on top of the fabric, so holding them with your left hand will keep them from springing up around the needle shaft. Hold them taut and to the left as you sink the needle into the background.

7. With the needle placed to the right of the appliqué (zig), lower the presser foot. Set the needle-down feature (if available). A down needle will keep everything in place anytime you need to stop to adjust the position.

Tap on the foot control to make zig and zag stitches, a stitch at a time. Steady pressure on the foot control will speed up stitching for continuous sewing. Keep your eyes on only the *right side of the folded edge,* guiding the fabric so the needle for the zig stitches enters the background precisely beside the edge. The machine will then place the zag stitch into the edge of the appliqué. If you have a speed control, set it to a slower rate until you gain confidence. **FIGURE C**

Zag stitch needle position

8. Take the zag stitch, which will be placed perfectly inside the edge of the appliqué. Stitch up a sample appliqué, trying out different adjustments to fine-tune your machine settings. **FIGURE D**

> *tip* On your appliqué sample, record your machine settings using a Pigma pen directly on the background fabric as you try various adjustments. Remove the piece from the machine and study the stitches in bright natural light to see which settings you prefer. Examine the back of the work, too.

Remember that the goal is balanced stitches. When closely inspecting your sample zigzag stitches, you should see only the clear polyester thread on the surface of the appliqué edges. **FIGURE E**

If you see tiny dots of cotton bobbin thread peeking out on top of the patch, you need to reduce the top thread tension because the top tension is pulling the bobbin stitches up to the surface.

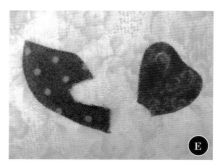

Correct tension

tip
Tension Tips

- *If the bobbin thread is showing on top of the appliqué, reduce the upper thread tension by moving the tension wheel to a lower number.*

- *If the monofilament is showing on the back of the work, increase the upper thread tension by moving the tension wheel to a higher number.*

- *After sewing an appliqué, examine the machine-appliquéd shape on the back of the work (the bobbin stitches are easier to see). A measurement of ⅛" from a zig stitch to the next zig stitch is a good standard length.*

 tip *When you're satisfied with the quality of your machine zigzag stitches, keep a written record for future reference. From here on out, you can begin machine appliqué with these established settings each time you sit down to sew, and you'll need to make only small adjustments as needed. Be aware that temperature and humidity are factors affecting the thread and fabric. Begin each sewing session by making a small sample so you can fine-tune your settings before sewing on your project.*

Be sure to try out a variety of appliqué shapes when you're practicing: inside and outside curves, straightaways, small and large circles, as well as inside and outside points.

Narrow zigzag stitches make the turning radius easy to navigate along wide inside and outside curves. Smaller or tighter shapes require you to stop with the needle down, lift, turn, and lower the presser foot. During practice, it will become apparent when you need to slow down or stop to readjust the foot because it will become harder to calculate the needle placement for the zig as you guide the edge into the stitch zone. The needle-down feature will lock in the position each time you stop to adjust or pivot the foot position. If this is not available on your machine, manually sink the needle down into the background fabric before pivoting.

As you gain control and skill, try reducing the width settings in small increments. The narrower the stitches, the less visible they'll be. Fabric color, weave, and print all play a role in whether you see needle holes or not. Also keep in mind that washing the project after appliquéing will make the top thread and needle holes less noticeable.

Machine Appliqué: Presser Foot Pivoting for Sharp Points

1. Sew zigzag stitches to within a single stitch of the point. Stop with zag needle down into the appliqué. **FIGURE F**

2. Lift the presser foot and manually insert the needle for a zig stitch precisely into the background at the tip, pivoting the appliqué toward the left. Line up the presser foot so the machine's next zag stitch will bring the needle straight across (right to left) to the inside of the appliqué point. **FIGURE G**

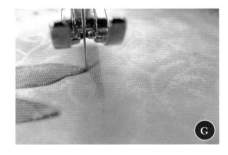

3. Lower the presser foot and execute the zag stitch inside the point. If your machine has a Pattern Begin function, use it to place the stitch. **FIGURE H**

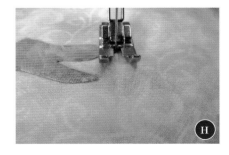

4. Lift the presser foot (not shown), pivoting the appliqué this time to face the point away from you. Lower the presser foot and continue to stitch along the other side of the point. **FIGURE I**

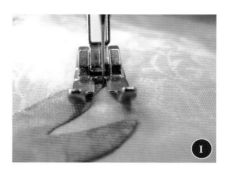

The same technique is used for deep V's and narrow inside and outside curves. The narrower the turning radius, the more stops and pivots you'll need to make.

A Note about Holes and Stitches

When you're machine appliquéing, you'll focus on every little stitch detail (which is a good thing for quality workmanship), but because you're zooming in for a close look, you might tend to be too critical, worrying about every needle hole or stitch. Let me put your mind at ease. When you add more appliqué pieces, embroidery, other embellished or dimensional elements, quilting on and around the motifs, and so on, the stitches and holes become less noticeable as the viewer's eyes gravitate toward more interesting elements. You'll never again give them a thought.

Tips on Stitching Common Shapes and Contours

Usually no stops are necessary for foot or needle adjustment when sewing around broad curves. For good stitch control, work at a reduced speed. From Marlene Chaffey's *Tiptoe through the Tulips* (page 52), created from *Hugs 'n' Kisses* design.

The tighter the curve, the more stops and pivots needed for accurate stitching. On tight curves, adjust stitch length closer so there are enough stitches to secure all edge work. Machine quilting on the background and between the appliqués brings them forward, adding dimension. From Mara Warwick's *Springtime's Promise* (page 83).

Reduce speed and stop only intermittently for presser foot and pivot adjustments on broader outside curves. More frequent stops are necessary for tighter inside curves. From *Tiptoe through the Tulips* by Marlene Chaffey (page 89).

Before glue-basting a piece with a deep V onto the background, you have the option to reinforce the inside clipped V area with permanent fabric glue. When stitching, stop with the needle down just before reaching the V to reset the zigzag stitch *length* to .30 (stitches very close together) for a few stitches in the center of the V. This will simulate thread wrapping (page 69), used to stabilize fragile areas in hand appliqué. Reset the stitch length to the usual setting to stitch the remainder of the piece. From Marlene Chaffey's *Tiptoe through the Tulips* (page 52).

The urn handle in *Hope Sings* requires stops and pivots at nearly every stitch to navigate the intricate profile. By Judy Shapiro (page 57).

With a very narrow stitch, you can generally sew right up to the tip on even the pointiest point (page 87). From Mara Warwick's *Springtime's Promise* (page 83).

For reverse appliqué, zigzag stitching is executed counterclockwise around the inside perimeter of the opening. Treat the fabric in the opening as background fabric. Start stitching on the left side of the opening with the needle down (zig) into the inside fabric and the zag stitches in the folded edge. For the elongated oval flutes shown, shorten the stitch length to .30 at the deep U shapes found at each end to securely thread-wrap vulnerable inside edges. From *Hope Sings* made by Judy Shapiro (page 57).

Tying Off Threads

I'm always disappointed when I see an otherwise fine example of machine appliqué sporting unsightly thread tail stubble popping up all over! A beautifully finished look is fast and easy to attain by bringing thread tails to the back of the work. For closed shapes, use tie off knots (pages 73 and 74) and hide the tails by embedding them between the background layer and appliqués. Clip the tails. For open shapes, clip the tails on the front since they will be overlapped by the next appliqué piece.

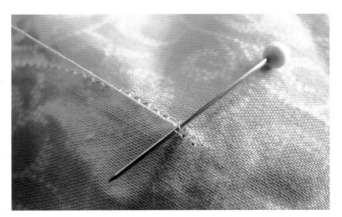

Working in Layers

Machine appliqué lends itself easily to working in layers. The machine is strong enough to allow the thin needle to penetrate many fabric layers without strain. Basting glue will ensure that pieces will not shift as you stitch. Gluing will also stiffen the edge of the appliqué for even stitching. Keeping the speed slow while stitching through layers will be kind to the needle and give you more control. In the F1 flower, the area where the flower center intersects the petals and leaf has a total of seven layers (three pieces each with turned edges plus the background fabric)—a lot of layers for the needle to penetrate! Sewing through all these layers was accomplished with ease at a slow pace.

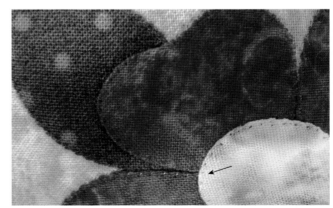

Off-Block Construction

Yet another way to machine appliqué is to preassemble a multipiece motif by first removing the freezer paper templates and then glue-basting the fabric appliqués together. The off-block gluing is completed *before* the design element is positioned as a whole unit onto the background. The whole motif is then positioned, glue-basted, and stitched to the background. This is an efficient way to prepare a motif, especially because the use of monofilament thread means you don't need to continually stop to change thread color. This technique is most helpful when working on very large projects because it requires only occasional use of the overlay for motif placement.

 *note* *For the detailed photo tutorial* Start to Finish: Machine Stitching an Appliqué Flower, *see page CD5.*

Basic Guidelines for Beautiful Machine Stitching

- Stabilize the background fabric with spray sizing (heat set with a hot, dry iron) before you begin to stitch on appliqués. Spray the front and back of the background, allowing the sizing to penetrate the fibers prior to pressing. Recheck the background registration marks against the overlay.

- Glue-baste the appliqués securely to the background fabric. This key to success provides a stiff edge for the needle to sew into and ensures that the appliqué will not shift. All glue will be washed out along with the sizing, so the soft hand of the fabric will return.

- Hold on to both threads as you take the first machine stitch to prevent the monofilament from springing back into the needle or the thread path, which can cause an aborted start.

- Stitch slowly for control and accuracy. You'll also minimize the risk of breaking a needle as you penetrate multiple layers of fabric. The 60/8 needles are very thin. You won't have a problem if you take your time.

- Sewing zig stitches too close to the appliqué edge can cause raggedy or scalloped-looking edges; sewing too far away will make the stitches and holes more visible. Your goal is to get your zig stitch to sink into the background just *next* to the folded edge.

- It's unnecessary to begin or end zigzag stitching with a machine knot (made by newer model machines) or a forward/backstitching sequence; both will add thread bulk. For open appliqués: Starts, stops, and raw edges will be covered and locked in when the next layer is appliquéd. Clip short all thread tails at the top of the work after stitching. For closed appliqués: Stitch past the beginning stitch with an extra stitch or two after coming full circle around the shape. Bring tails to the back and tie off. Bury the tails between the appliqué and the background.

- Avoid a mess of stray threads on the back of your work by taking the background out from the machine after you complete each closed appliqué.

- If you notice the monofilament jerking rather than feeding smoothly through the top thread path of your machine, try removing the spool from the vertical spool pin and, instead, placing the spool in a small bowl resting on the work surface behind the machine.

- For frequent presser-foot adjustments during small-radius curves, you might prefer to use a knee-operated, hands-free presser-foot lifter, available on some machines.

- Work in bright light!

- For larger projects, roll up the excess background fabric to keep the bulk from interfering as you sew.

Congratulations! You now have all the skills necessary for beautiful turned-edge appliqué by machine! You're ready for any project you set your sights on.

Finishing

You've put your heart and soul into your beautiful appliqué, so it deserves the very best finishing treatment. Finishing includes washing (optional, but reccommended), soft pressing, and squaring-up.

Washing Finished Appliqué

Hand Washing

1. Fill a sink or wash basin with a gallon of tepid tap water. Add a few drops of Synthrapol (or alternative, such as inexpensive shampoo or Woolite—but check that no brighteners are added). Stir well. (For larger pieces adjust quantity up to ½ teaspoon per gallon.)

2. Add half of a Shout Color Catcher sheet.

3. Place the appliqué in the water, dipping gently until well saturated. Allow it to soak at least 10 minutes, agitating gently by hand intermittently.

4. Rinse well in cool water.

5. Air dry flat on a clean, dry towel.

Machine Washing

1. Set the washing machine to the delicate cycle using warm-water wash and cool rinse. NOTE: I set the dial forward so that the wash cycle is half the usual amount of time.

2. Place ¼ teaspoon of Synthrapol (or alternative, such as inexpensive shampoo or Woolite—but check that no brighteners are added) in the detergent dispenser or wash drum (depending on your washer).

3. Place the appliqué in a mesh bag and load into the washer with half of a Shout Color Catcher sheet and several pieces of muslin (or other white cotton fabric) so the washer contents agitate well (without sticking to the sides of the drum). When the cycle is completed, remove the appliqué.

4. Air dry flat on a clean, dry towel.

Soft Pressing

Soft pressing as you work on appliqué is important for several reasons, and doing it correctly is crucial to the appearance of the work. Soft pressing is done on a specially prepared lofty surface, which gives the benefit of flattening the background while protecting any dimensional appliqué elements or raised embroidery stitches. Turned-edge appliqué has a slightly raised edge that is appealing, and you want to preserve the look of that subtle dimensional effect. Remember, pressing means just that—the iron is lowered onto and lifted off the fabric surface. It is not ironed with a back-and-forth motion. Wash out any washable marker lines before pressing.

How to Soft Press

GATHER:

- 1 or more clean, dry fluffy bath towels (preferably white or cream color)
- Clean white T-shirt (the larger the better) *or* a yard of white cotton flannel
- Iron set to cotton with steam
- Hard pressing board
- Finished appliqué block

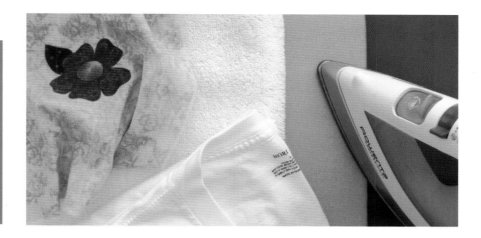

1. Place the towel folded in layers on the hard pressing board and smooth the T-shirt on top. Position the appliqué block facedown on top of the prepared soft pressing surface. The T-shirt will provide a smoother surface than the bumpy terry loops on the towel. **FIGURE A**

2. Steam press (iron up and down, not back and forth) all areas of the block until the background is smooth—without creases, wrinkles, or puckers. The dimensional elements will sink down into the soft fluffy surface when the background is pressed flat. When you lift up the appliqué block, you'll notice indentations on the surface of the T-shirt—impressions made by the raised features of the appliqué. Examine the appliqué and background from the front side. The appliqué will boast subtle raised edges, the dimensional elements will be sitting up proud and high, and the background will lie nice and flat! **FIGURE B**

3. Check the pressed block against the overlay registration marks. Make any necessary adjustments at this time by dampening, coaxing the block square, and pressing it again.

When to Press

Appliqué will benefit from several soft pressings on the way to completing the project.

Soft Pressing along the Way

As a natural consequence of sewing on appliqué pieces, the fabric is drawn in a bit with each stitch (even if you use the proper tension). You may notice after a while that the registration marks on the background don't match up with those on the overlay. Soft pressing will help to even out the appliqué and background so they realign with the registration marks. For simpler designs, this may not be necessary; but for elaborate designs with many layers, two or three soft pressings over the course of making the block will be a big help in keeping it true.

Soft Pressing before Embroidery Embellishment

If you are planning to add embroidered details to your appliqué, soft pressing the block before you begin will provide you with a perfect surface upon which to execute beautifully formed embroidery stitches. While you are pressing, be certain to check that the registration marks are straight. If they are not, use a steam setting to help encourage the block back into alignment.

Soft Pressing upon Completion

During the process of appliqué and embellishing, the block is handled quite a bit. Careful as you may be, your piece will likely have a rumpled look by the time it is completed. Soft pressing the finished block will freshen up the background and puff up all dimensional work, making it look neat and tidy. Additionally, a final pressing is done to make the block as square as possible in readiness for trimming (squaring) it to size.

Squaring (Truing) the Block after Completion

After the completed appliqué block is pressed, the background fabric will need to be squared or trued up to its vertical and horizontal lines and trimmed down to its exact finished size. The finished size is the desired size of the block plus ¼″ added to each side for seam allowances.

If you're planning to use the appliqué block immediately, to set it into a quilt or other project, it can be trimmed now. However, if you're not quite ready to use the finished block, it's best to leave the registration stitches in place and not cut the excess fabric from the edges. Trimmed edges fray easily. Instead, store your blocks-in-waiting with a layer of fluffy batting between them or rolled (good side out) around a swimming pool noodle covered with washed muslin. This will keep your creations safe and dust free. Then, just prior to sewing, you can make freshly cut, accurate edges on the block.

Squaring Method 1: Layered Appliqué Blocks

For single-layer appliqué designs that do not have dimensional elements, the job of squaring the final block is a simple task. Use a cutting mat, large square quilter's ruler, and rotary cutter for an accurate cut. The registration marks have been true and reliable from the start of the project, so matching them up now with the vertical and horizontal lines on the ruler and mat will ensure that your appliqué is centered and the finished background size is accurate.

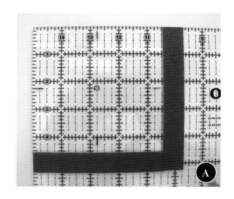

1. The finished size of the sample flower block needs to be 4½″ × 4½″ (that's 4″ for the block itself, plus ¼″ seam allowance on each side). Beginning at a corner of the square ruler, tape off a 4½″ square with painter's tape (leaving a *sliver* of space around the grid lines so you can see the ruler markings). This will identify the area that your background block will fill, making it visually distinct and eliminating any chance for error. **FIGURE A**

2. Using a washable marker, identify the halfway point on each side of the square (in this case the total size equals 4½″, so halfway would be 2¼″). With the halfway point marked on 2 of the sides, mark the center of the square with a circle where the side markings intersect, and mark the halfway point on the remaining 2 sides of the taped square. Set the ruler aside. **FIGURE B**

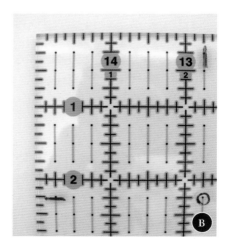

3. Working on the gridded side of a cutting mat, match the registration marks on the background fabric to vertical and horizontal lines on the mat (any lines will do). This will ensure that your background is squared-up. Tape the background corners to the mat with drafting tape to prevent the block from shifting. Disregard outside edges of the background fabric. **FIGURE C**

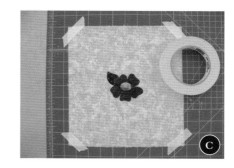

4. Line up the registration marks on the background with the halfway marks on the ruler. With a rotary cutter, trim the first 2 sides of the block, using the ruler edge as the cutting guide to create a cut corner. **FIGURE D**

5. Rotate the block 180°, lining up the block cut corner inside the guidelines of the taped ruler corner. Use the ruler edges as a cutting guide to trim off the remaining 2 sides, completing the 4½″ block. NOTE: Placing the ruler on top of the block protects the work in case the cutter slips.

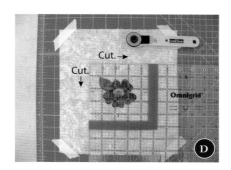

Squaring Method 2: Dimensional Appliqué Blocks

When dimensional elements or raised embroidery stitches are worked into an appliqué design, a square quilter's ruler can't be used. The ruler will wobble and shift instead of lying flat, making cutting inaccurate and squishing the beautiful dimensional details on your block! Instead, make and use a window-style cutting guide.

Use illustration board to make a frame or window for the dimensional block, allowing the appliqué to be centered precisely while the raised elements remain undisturbed. All the calculations and measurements are done on the illustration board first, so any mistakes are made on the board and not your precious block!

GATHER:
- Illustration board (¹⁄₁₆″ thick, available at office supply or craft stores)
- Disposable retractable cutting blade (at paint and wallpaper stores)
- Mechanical pencil
- 18″ or longer quilter's ruler
- Gridded cutting mat
- Drafting tape

1. The finished size of the sample flower block needs to be 4½″ × 4½″ (4″ for the block itself, plus ¼″ seam allowance on each side). Add 2″ on each side (for the frame), making the total an 8½″ × 8½″ square.

2. Cut the illustration board into a square that is 8½″ × 8½″. Tape the board to the cutting mat. Using a ruler and mat, draw a pencil line grid on the illustration board as follows: Draw horizontal lines across the board at 2″, 4¼″, and 6½″ from the edge. Repeat, drawing vertical lines at 2″, 4½″, and 6½″ from the edge. **FIGURE E**

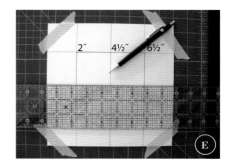

3. Cut out and remove the center 4½″ × 4½″ square from the board, using a ruler and cutting blade, creating a window with registration marks. Hint: Several passes using light pressure on the blade will work better than a single pass using strong pressure. **FIGURE F**

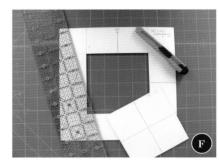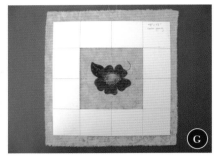

4. Match the registration marks on the board with those on the background fabric. **FIGURE G**

5. Inside each window corner, use a mechanical pencil to mark a dot. **FIGURE H**

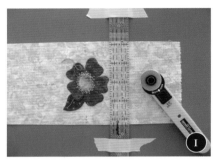

6. A side at a time, line up the corner dots with a ruler. Trim off the excess fabric without cutting off the dots. Placing a narrow ruler to the inside of the cutting line will protect the block in case the blade slips. Taping the ruler will help anchor it as you cut. Recommended order of cutting: left side, right side, top, and bottom. NOTE: Leaving these marked dots on the fabric accomplishes 2 things: After trimming the first 2 sides (left and right) the pencil marks will still be there to line up the ruler for the last 2 side cuts, *and* your block will be finished to the exact size. **FIGURE I**

7. Leave the registration marks (stitches) in place on the block. You'll find these helpful if you're attaching sashing or borders. Stitches can easily be removed after the project is assembled. NOTE: The photos sometimes show bowing on straight edges because of the camera lens (or the cockeyed photographer, me), but the actual block is straight and accurate! **FIGURE J**

Special Appliqué Techniques

Dimensional Flowers

Gathered Petals

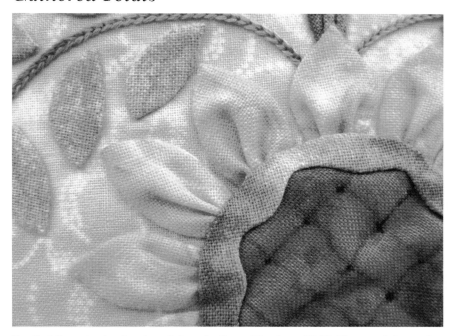

Detail of dimensional gathered petals from *Sunflower Glory* (page CD50). These petals have points but are made the same as rounded-tip petals.

GATHER:
- Prepared petal appliqué
- Background fabric
- Overlay
- Sequin pins
- Embroidery needle
- Heavyweight thread
- Scissors
- Embroidery needle
- Appliqué needle
- Appliqué thread

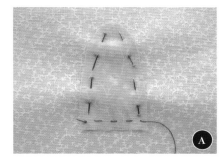

1. With heavyweight thread, sew running stitches ⅛″ from the raw edge of a prepared petal. Pin-baste the appliqué onto the background fabric, using the overlay for placement. **FIGURE A**

2. With fine thread, appliqué around the top half of the petal. Tie off the appliqué thread at the back of the work, and remove the basting pins. Rethread the hanging tail of the gathering thread. Gently draw in the bottom edge of petal into gathered pleats. Tackstitch the gathered edge securely to the background, and tie off the gathering thread at the back of the work. **FIGURE B**

3. Pin-baste the petal, shaping the sides. Appliqué the lower sides to finish the petal. Remove the pins. Tie off the threads at the back of the work. **FIGURE C**

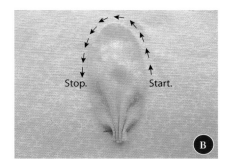

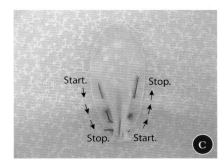

Folded Flower Bud

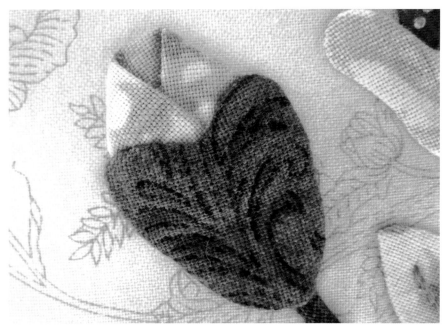

GATHER:
- Fabric for flower bud
- Scissors
- Quilting or heavy cotton thread
- Embroidery needle
- Circle template *or* circle template maker
- Pencil

Dimensional folded flower bud as seen in *Tweet Treats* (fancy version, page 123)

1. Use a freezer paper circle template or a commercial circle template to trace the circle onto the fabric. Cut it out.

2. Fold the circle in half, right sides out.

3. Fold over the top left corner, angled toward the right. Pin to hold. **FIGURE A**

4. Fold over the top right corner, angled toward the left. Pin to hold.

5. Sew running stitches about ¼″ from the bottom edge; then remove the pins.

6. Pull the thread tightly to form gathers in the bottom edge. Take a backstitch at the left edge to hold the gathers. NOTE: Excess fabric bulk may be trimmed below the stitching line. Tackstitch the bud in place and appliqué a calyx to cover raw edges. **FIGURE B**

Pleated Fan Blossom

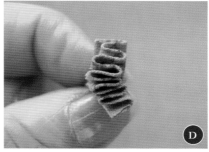

Pleated fan blossom as seen in *A Basketful of Hope* (classic color plan, page CD65)

1. Using the template, cut the fabric for the fan strip on the bias and preturn the bottom (long) edge and sides. Preturn the appliqué bract as usual. Remove the freezer paper templates. **FIGURE C**

2. Fold the strip in an accordion style, making narrow pleats. Gather and pinch the raw edge. NOTE: Fold the strip so the first and last folds will turn under. **FIGURE D**

3. Flatten the fan folds. **FIGURE E**

GATHER:
- Fabric for fan strip and bract
- Strip and bract templates
- Background fabric
- Overlay
- Heavyweight thread
- Scissors
- Embroidery needle
- Appliqué needle
- Fine thread
- Sequin pins or basting glue

4. Audition a preturned bract on top of the pinched folds, adjusting the fan to fit inside the bract edges. **FIGURE F**

5. Backstitch across the raw edges to secure the folds. Tie off and allow the folded edge to fan out. Press the stitched edge with a hot, dry iron. **FIGURE G**

6. Make sure the bract will cover the raw edges. Place the blossom on the background fabric, using the overlay. Pin or glue-baste the blossom in position. Anchor the fan, using hidden tack stitches inside the fan folds ¼″ from the stitched edge. Appliqué the fan sides to the background. Allow the folds to stand up for added dimension. Appliqué the bract piece on top of the fan blossom.

Puff Blossom

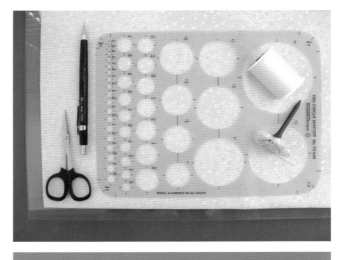

Cluster of dimensional five-petal puff blossoms embellished with French knot centers, from *A Basketful of Hope* (page 124)

GATHER:
- Circle master pattern
- Quilting or heavy-weight thread in color to match blossom fabric
- Embroidery needle
- Scissors
- Mechanical pencil
- Lapboard
- Fabric for blossoms

1. Cut out a circle; see Puff Blossom Size Chart (page 101) or the project circle template (page CD82).

2. Stitch around the circle with running stitches ⅛″ from the edge. Be sure to knot the thread so the knot won't pull through the fabric. Pull the thread through every few stitches. Keep the stitches even and consistent. **FIGURE A**

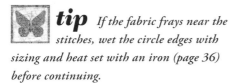 ***tip*** *If the fabric frays near the stitches, wet the circle edges with sizing and heat set with an iron (page 36) before continuing.*

3. As you approach the knot, plan ahead to take a down stitch into the same hole as the knot and emerge a single stitch beyond

the knot (using a shared hole). This will make a smoother circle join and ease strain on the knot. **FIGURE B**

4. Pull the thread through; continue pulling the thread slowly to draw up the circle edges into a puff, working to evenly distribute the gathers. Placing your left index fingertip inside the puff while tugging on the thread will help. **FIGURE C**

5. Turn the puff gathered side up, pulling the thread tightly until the gathers come together to make a center hole. Use the needle to manipulate the gathers evenly. Flatten the puff into a yo-yo shape, coaxing the hole to sit at the center of the puff circle. Use overcast stitches to secure the gathers and control fraying. **FIGURE D**

6. Insert the needle through the center hole at the back, emerging on the front side of the puff. **FIGURE E**

7. Pull the thread through tightly to create the first gathered indentation (the beginning of a sculpted petal). **FIGURE F**

8. Bring the needle around to the back again, inserting the needle point through the center using the same hole. As you pull the needle through, begin to adjust the position of the thread as it forms an overcast loop. **FIGURE G**

9. Move the loop slightly to the right of the first indentation (as you tighten it) to create a second gathered indentation, making the first petal. NOTE: Do not be overly concerned that the petals are evenly spaced—part of nature's charm is that each flower is a bit different. **FIGURE H**

10. Continue in this manner until all 5 petals are formed. Insert needle into center, pulling it through to the back. Make 1 or 2 overcast stitches on the back and tie off. **FIGURE I**

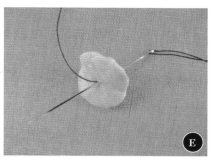

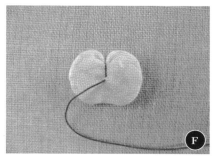

11. Glue-baste the flowers in place on the background fabric. Sew permanently in place using hidden tack stitches (page 70) around the flower perimeter ⅛″ inside the edge.

tip
Puff Blossom Tips

- *Planning your overcast stitch placement around the edge of the puff can result in a three-, four-, or five-petal puff blossom. You have the option to make an even, consistent arrangement of petals or an uneven petal arrangement, with each flower taking on a unique look.*

- *Every fabric works up differently. Lightweight, meaty, washed (softer), and so on all influence how the gathers and petals fall into place.*

- *Try turning the finished blossom over and using the back side as the front. Sometimes the gathers take on an interesting look. But you'll need to overcast the center with matching thread several times (to tame the fraying) and carefully clip off any stray fabric threads. Then use clusters of French knots (made with perle cotton) to cover the center, hiding the messy part.*

- *Variation: Use strong thread to make the gathered circle, tying off on back. Use embroidery floss or perle cotton to add the petal indentations.*

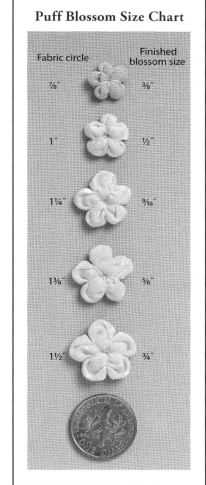

Puff Blossom Size Chart

Fabric circle	Finished blossom size
⅞″	⅜″
1″	½″
1¼″	9⁄16″
1⅜″	⅝″
1½″	¾″

Circular Ruched Blossom

A template pattern is provided on the CD for all ruched blossoms in the projects. Use a lightbox to transfer the cutting lines and dots that are the stitching guides. NOTE: *Ruch* is pronounced "roosh." A Ruche Mark ruching guide is available for other size blossoms.

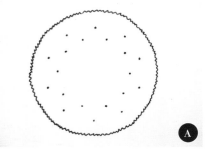

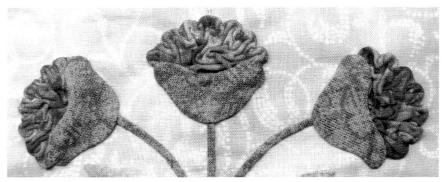

Partial ruched blossoms from *Sunflower Glory* (page CD50)

Fold connects the dots

Partial Ruched Blossoms

1. Transfer all the markings from the ruching template pattern onto the right side of the fabric. The outermost circle (zigzag line) is the cutting line. There is an outside circle of dots and an inside circle of dots, which (if connected) form a zigzag pattern. **FIGURE A**

2. Identify 2 dots (any 2 dots) from the *outside* circle of dots. Roll the outer edge of the fabric away from you, folding the fabric in a straight line to connect the 2 dots. NOTE: The fold-over becomes the turned seam allowance. **FIGURE B**

3. Insert a needle threaded with heavyweight thread up inside the fold, emerging at the right dot. Pull the thread through to bury the knot in the fold seam.

4. Connect the outside dots to the inside dots using small running stitches, forming a series of zigzag lines around the circle edge. **FIGURE C**

5. Each time you emerge at an outside dot, stop to roll back a turn-under allowance (in a straight line) between the dot where the thread is emerging and the next outside dot. When you look at the back of the work, you will see that the excess fabric in the turned edge is forming pleats and gathers as you stitch. The last up stitch should emerge from an inside dot. **FIGURE D**

GATHER:
- Fabric for blossoms and calyx
- Circle and calyx templates
- Scissors
- Iron
- Heavyweight thread
- Chalk marker
- Embroidery needle
- Sequin pins
- Background fabric
- Overlay

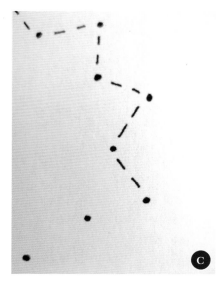

6. Continue stitching until the thread emerges at an outside dot and only 2 outside dots and 3 inside dots remain. Stop here because this ruched blossom is a partial flower, so stitching around the entire circle perimeter is not needed. **FIGURE E**

7. Pull up the thread tightly, adjusting gathers into evenly spaced scallops around the edge. Press the blossom flat with your fingers. Adjust the perimeter size by tightening or loosening the thread to fit the blossom size on the master pattern. **FIGURE F**

8. Press the blossom flat with your fingertips. Use the overlay to position the blossom on the background fabric and pin-baste the top edge in place (not shown). Stitch the top outside edge to the background using hidden tack stitches (page 70) in the folds of the edge scallops. Tie off on the back. Remove the basting pins and use your fingertips and an awl point to adjust the inside gathers, distributing the excess fabric evenly into nooks and crannies. Fold under the left and right bottom edges of the blossom, pinning them in place (shown). **FIGURE G**

9. Audition the prepared calyx appliqué on top of the blossom, making certain the calyx covers the ruched flower sides. Ignore the fabric protruding at the bottom edge. Set the calyx aside. Adjust the ruched fabric folds, pinning as needed. **FIGURE H**

10. When satisfied with the blossom folds, use hidden tack stitches between the fabric folds to hold them in place permanently. NOTE: Do not pull too tightly on the tack stitches; this will cause your background fabric to pucker. After the folds are stitched in place, sew a line of running backstitches below the gathered (ruched) area. Remove the pins and trim off the excess bottom fabric, ⅛″ below the running stitches.

11. Use the overlay to position the calyx. Pin-baste the calyx on top of the ruched blossom. If you are hand appliquéing, sew the calyx in place using stab stitches (pages 65–67), especially in areas where the calyx is layered on top of dimensional ruching.

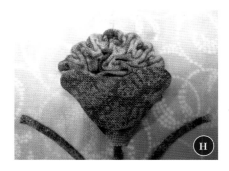

Full Circular Ruched Blossoms

Circular ruched blossom from *Hope Sweet Hope* (page CD103)

1. For a complete circular ruched blossom, follow the partial blossom instructions (pages 102 and 103) through Step 6, but stitch around the entire perimeter of the circle until you return to the beginning stitch, ending with the needle up and emerging at an outside dot (in a shared hole).

2. Pull up tightly on the thread, teasing the gathers into evenly spaced scallops around the edge. Concentrate on pressing the edges flat with your fingers to form a circle (ignore the puff of excess fabric in the center for now). Adjust the blossom perimeter by tightening or loosening the thread to fit the flower outline size on the master pattern. Lock in the size of the ruched circle with a hidden backstitch.

3. Use the overlay to position the blossom on the background. Pin-baste it in place and then stitch around the blossom perimeter with tack stitches (page 70) hidden in the folds of the scalloped edges. Tie off the thread and remove the basting pins.

4. Use the point of an awl to coax the excess center fabric into gathers, evenly forming nooks and crannies to ease in all the fabric fullness. Press flat with your fingertips. When you are satisfied with the blossom folds, hold the folds in place with your left thumb.

5. Bring a threaded needle to the front of the work. Use hidden tack stitches between the fabric folds to hold them in place permanently. Don't pull the tack stitches too tightly to prevent background puckering. Expect the back of the work to show a series of thread crossovers, as the folds are stitched permanently in place. When the folds are secure, tie off the thread at the back of the work.

Double-Double Pressed Skinny Stems

Tweet Treats (page 123) boasts a lot of simple, curved stems.

This method makes perfect little ⅛″-wide bias stems.

> **GATHER:**
> - Hard pressing board
> - Hot, dry iron
> - Spray sizing in small bowl
> - #1 or #2 round paintbrush
> - Precut bias fabric strips ⅞″ wide

1. With the brush, run a line of liquid sizing down the center of the bias strip. **FIGURE A**

2. Fold the strip lengthwise, matching the edges. Heat press the fold down the length of the strip. The strip will be a double fabric layer. If the fold is not sharp, resize the fold and heat set again. **FIGURE B**

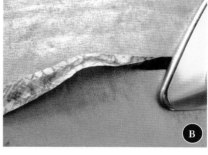

3. Run a line of sizing down the center of the doubled strip. NOTE: When working with longer strips, apply sizing in small increments.

4. Fold the strip lengthwise in half again, positioning the folded edge to cover the raw edges a tad. Press the strip to heat set the new folded edge. The double strip is now doubled again. Make certain all edges are crisp and lie flat. You may need to resize and press the folds again. **FIGURE C**

Using Double-Double Pressed Stems

1. Place the overlay on the background, lining up the registration marks. Working *on top* of the overlay, cut a length of the double-double stem to match the size of a stem on the master pattern, adding ¼″ seam allowances to each stem end so the appliqué flowers and leaves will cover them. Shape the stem (remember it is bendable!) to the curve of the design. **FIGURE D**

2. Flip the stem to the wrong side (not shown) and place dots of basting glue along it at intervals. Pick up the stem with tweezers and insert it *beneath* the overlay, aligning the stem with the stem design line. **FIGURE E**

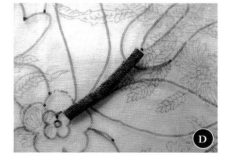

 tip *You can glue-baste one stem at a time or several before stitching them down.*

3. Remove the overlay and press to set the basting glue. You're ready to appliqué the stem in place on the background. If appliquéing by hand, a stab stitch (pages 65–67) will work best because of the dimensional stem's multiple fabric layers.

tip *For ¼″-wide stems, use a bias tape maker. Follow the manufacturer's directions for cutting the bias strips. Here's my method for great results: Apply sizing to the sides of the strip with a brush before you insert the strip into the tool. Then be sure to slant the iron to make a broader heat-setting surface. Let the left hand guide but not pull the bias tape maker. Use the iron to push the tool tip along as it heat sets the emerging strip.*

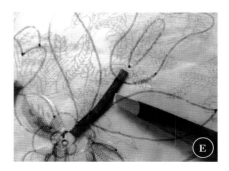

Dimensional Elements

The special details in your appliqué matter. They elevate a piece from very fine to exceptional. Bird eggs, ladybugs, and berries all make wonderful surprises for viewers to enjoy, but creating them as dimensional elements makes them even more enticing.

Dimensional Berries

Clusters of berries always draw our attention in nature, and they'll offer a sweet addition to the foliage in your appliqué, too. One way to add berries is to embroider them with padded satin stitches (page 119). They're fast and easy to execute, resulting in a slightly raised embellishment. Below are two different types of dimensional appliqué berries: foundation berries and stuffed berries. NOTE: For beginning berry makers, start with a larger berry to gain control over the method and then move on to smaller and smaller berries.

Foundation Berries

GATHER:

- Fabric for berries
- Stiff interfacing / Patch Back (page 8)
- Elmer's Washable School Glue Stick
- Scrap copy paper
- Scissors
- Tweezers
- Lapboard
- Variety of pointy tools (awl, cuticle stick, toothpick, pearl-head pin)
- Freezer paper berry template patterns or plastic circle template
- Mechanical pencil
- Iron

Foundation berries from *A Basketful of Hope* (page CD65)

1. Prepare freezer-paper berry templates and iron them onto stiff interfacing/Patch Back foundation (page 8) or use a plastic circle template to trace the berries onto the foundation. Cut out the foundation berries and remove the templates. For these instructions, 2 layers of foundation are used. Use more layers for berries with added height. **FIGURE A**

 *tip* *If you are making a lot of berries, print the circle template patterns directly onto stiff interfacing/Patch Back using an inkjet printer.*

2. Place a berry foundation on scrap paper (to protect work surfaces). Use a gluestick to apply glue to a side of the berry foundation.

3. With tweezers, lift the glued foundation off the paper and place it sticky side down onto the wrong side of the berry fabric. Use tweezers to glue and stack a second berry foundation on top of the first. **FIGURE B**

4. Cut out the fabric, adding ⅛″ beyond the edge of the foundation berry for turn-over allowance. **FIGURE C**

 *tip* *When working with small berries, a rule of thumb is to add edge fabric cut to half the width of the circle, so that as the fabric is turned over the edges of the foundation, the fabric will not go past the center of the circle and cause too much bulk.*

5. Working on paper, apply an even layer of glue on top of both the foundation and fabric berry. Pick up the glued berry with tweezers and move it to a clean spot on the paper.

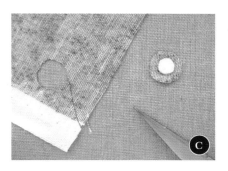

6. Begin to turn over the fabric edges—you'll need 2 pointed tools: a tool for holding the berry and a tool for turning over the fabric edges. Try different tools to see which you handle best. I find that the combination of a cuticle stick (to hold the berry) and an awl (to fold over the tiny fabric edge gathers) works best for me. **FIGURE D**

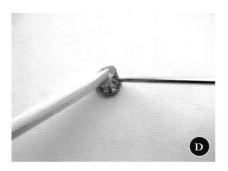

7. Glue-baste the berry in place on the background fabric, using the overlay for placement. Appliqué the berry using stab stitches (pages 65–67) hidden on the underside of the perimeter. **FIGURE E**

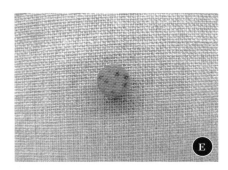

Stuffed Berries

Dimensional stuffed berries from *Springtime's Promise* (page CD122)

GATHER:

- Fabric for berries
- 100% natural wool roving (preferred) *or* 100% wool yarn cut into bits and shredded
- Embroidery needle
- Quilting or heavyweight cotton thread (to match)
- Chalk marking pencil
- Freezer paper berry templates *or* circle template
- Scissors
- Toothpick
- Cuticle stick
- Lapboard
- Pressing board
- Iron

1. Heat set a freezer paper circle template to the right side of the fabric, or cut out a circle template and use the window to fussy cut (pages 25 and 26) a berry. Cut out the fabric circle and remove the freezer paper. Alternatively, use a circle template to trace a circle with a chalk pencil; then cut it out.

2. With the fabric circle right side up, bring a threaded needle up from beneath the circle. Taking 2 running stitches at a time ⅛″ from the edge, stitch around the perimeter, ending a single stitch past the starting stitch. **FIGURE A**

3. Pull up the thread slightly to form a puff shape, leaving a well on the underside between the gathers.

4. Pinch off a tiny bit of wool fiber. Stuff the wool fiber into the berry opening. Continue to coax and stuff the fiber inside the berry until it is quite hard. Try using the cuticle stick initially and then change to a toothpick as the berry gets close to full. A full, packed berry will feel quite hard. **FIGURE B**

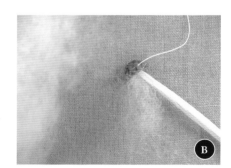

5. Inspect the stuffed berry from the top. If it is fully stuffed, it will be round and dense with no fabric wrinkles around the sides. **FIGURE C**

6. Insert the threaded needle point ⅛″ inside the raw gathered edges at 6:00, emerge at 12:00, and pull the needle and thread through tightly. Continue to take overcast stitches, working around the berry—7:00 to 1:00, 8:00 to 2:00, 9:00 to 3:00, and so forth—until the raw edges are encased in thread wraps. **FIGURE D**

tip *Leave the thread tail attached to the berry so it can be used to anchor it to the background. Tie off the heavy thread at the back of the work. Resume attaching the berry using fine-weight thread, taking hidden stab stitches (pages 65–67) beneath the berry base. Tie off.*

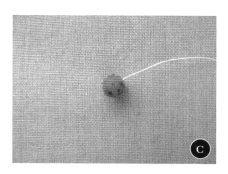

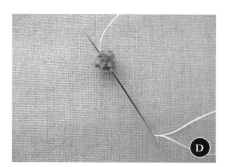

Stuffed Eggs and Ladybugs

Stuffed Eggs

Dimensional stuffed eggs from *Springtime's Promise* (page CD122)

GATHER:
- Fabric for eggs (a themed print works great but isn't necessary)
- 100% wool roving (or wool yarn cut into bits and shredded)
- Freezer-paper egg template patterns from project patterns
- Scissors
- Matching-colored fine thread (silk is strong without adding bulk)
- Appliqué needle
- Cuticle stick
- Toothpick

NOTE: Contrasting thread is used in these instructions.

1. Begin with a preturned appliqué egg, with the template removed, ready to stitch.

2. Pin-baste the egg appliqué to the background fabric. Appliqué around the perimeter. Hand appliquérs should use stab stitches very close together (pages 65–67); use a reduced stitch length for machine appliqué. The stuffing will put strain on the stitches, so it is important that they have a good hold at every edge to maintain a smooth egg shape. Continue stitching around the egg, leaving a small unstitched opening. Bring the needle and thread to the back of the work, parking the needle off to the side. **FIGURE A**

3. Pinch off a small amount of wool fiber. Stuff it into the opening with a cuticle stick; change to a toothpick as the egg fills. Push the fiber toward the opposite side of the egg, overstuffing it until it feels hard to the touch. **FIGURE B**

4. Hold down the open edge with your thumb as you bring the needle and thread back up to the surface, taking stab stitches to close the opening. Continue to squeeze the edge closed with your thumb, stitching the opening completely closed, adding 1 or 2 stitches beyond the first stitch. Tie off snugly at the back of the work. **FIGURE C**

5. Use the needle point to redistribute the fiber so the egg is evenly stuffed to a nice oval shape. **FIGURE D**

Stuffed Ladybug

Dimensional stuffed ladybugs are nothing more than stuffed eggs made with red fabric and embroidered with black floss details.

Dimensional stuffed ladybug from *Sunflower Glory* (page CD50)

Reverse Appliqué

Reverse appliqué is a snap wirth Simply Successful Appliqué. It uses the same basic techniques but adds appliqué to the *inside* of an appliqué shape, like a donut hole. An appliqué ring (page 42 and 43) is actually a reverse appliqué motif!

Reverse appliqué nest from *Springtime's Promise* (page CD122)

1. Cut out the center of the freezer paper appliqué template where the reverse appliqué detail will appear.

2. Preturn the outside edges where the appliqué will show; the remaining raw edges will be covered by other appliqué pieces. Preturning the outside edges first helps to stabilize the fabric, making it easy to cut out the inside fabric and turn the edges. **FIGURE E**

3. Cut out the center fabric, adding a ⅛″ turn-under allowance. **FIGURE F**

4. Turn and heat set the edges with an iron as you would any other appliqué.

5. Hand or machine appliqué.

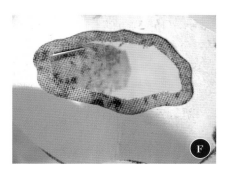

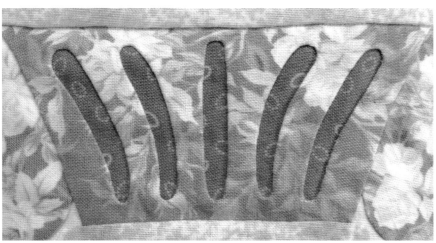

The flutes on the vase in *Hope Sings* (page CD89) are created using reverse appliqué.

Lined Appliqué

The most common need for lining an appliqué is to prevent shadowing, the unwelcome effect of color showing through a fabric when the fabric below it is darker.

GATHER:
- Prepared appliqué to be lined
- Fusible interfacing or Shadow Block lining
- Small piece of lightweight cotton (or pressing cloth)
- Mechanical pencil
- Scissors
- Iron
- Hard pressing board
- Lapboard

The light pink ribbon in *A Basketful of Hope* (page CD73) is lined to prevent shadowing.

1. Remove the freezer paper template from a preturned appliqué that needs to be lined. Set the piece aside. **FIGURE A**

2. Flip the template shiny side up and place it on the fusible side of the fusible interfacing (the side with the sheen). Trace around the template edge with a mechanical pencil. **FIGURE B**

3. Cut out around the perimeter of the traced shape, trimming off ⅛″ inside all the traced lines to reduce the size of the lining. **FIGURE C**

4. Center the lining, fusible side down, inside the turned edges of the prepared appliqué shape. **FIGURE D**

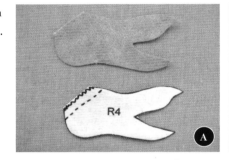

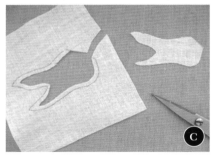

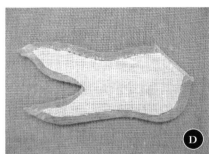

5. On a hard pressing surface, place a pressing cloth on top of the layered appliqué/lining piece. With the iron set to steam and wool, press on the pressing cloth for 10–12 seconds. Press again on the right side of the appliqué (using a pressing cloth) for 6–8 seconds. Allow it to cool, and it's ready to appliqué. NOTE: When pressing, be sure to *press* and not *iron* back and forth.

 tip *Audition the piece on the background where it will appear, checking to see if the lining provides sufficient coverage. If not, a second layer of lining may be needed.*

Other Lining Situations

- When working with very thin or flimsy fabric, the lining will serve to stabilize an appliqué for easier handling and to minimize skewing or stretching of the shape.
- Use lining when working with light or translucent fabrics where you can see the preturned seam allowances shadowing through to the top of the appliqué.
- Use lining when you notice that the color of an appliqué becomes tinted by the color of the fabric below it.

Needle Trapunto

Trapunto is a technique used to add texture and dimension to quilts by padding or stuffing design elements. Needle trapunto is an easy way to add this impressive look to your appliqué. The technique is the same for any shape.

The raised effect (relief) of the bird wing from *Tweet Treats* (page CD36) is created with the needle trapunto technique.

GATHER:

- Completed appliqué project
- Scissors
- Doll or soft sculpture needle
- Medium-weight 100% wool yarn
- Lapboard

1. Select an appliqué element you would like to trapunto. For this lesson, a circle appliqué is featured for simplicity. The technique is the same for any shape. **FIGURE E**

2. Thread a doll needle with a length of yarn.

3. The first trapunto stitch will be placed across the center of the shape (outlined by the stitches) by dividing the shape in half visually. Holding the needle horizontally, insert needle (right to left) *between* the background layer of fabric and the appliqué layer, making certain to stay inside the perimeter of stitches. Check from the front of the work to make sure the needle did not penetrate the surface. **FIGURE F**

4. Pull the yarn through until a 1″ tail remains. Clip the yarn on the other side, also leaving a 1″ tail.

5. Insert the needle again, a yarn width above the first yarn stitch, and add another strand of yarn as before. **FIGURE G**

6. Continue alternating sides until the entire shape is filled with yarn. **FIGURE H**

7. Carefully clip off all the tails close to the background surface, a tail at a time, after the shape is filled. **FIGURE I**

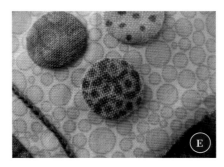

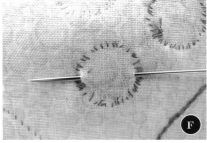

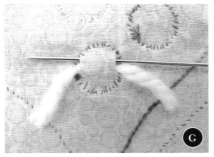

Broderie Perse

Broderie Perse translates literally as "Persian embroidery," but as we use it today it refers to the special appliqué technique of cutting out around the perimeter of a printed fabric motif and turning the edges so it can be appliquéd onto a background. From a distance, the appliqués appear to be amazingly detailed.

Broderie Perse roses from *Tweet Treats* (page CD36)

GATHER:
- Lightbox
- Fabric with motif for Broderie Perse
- Freezer paper
- Mechanical pencil
- Scissors
- Hard pressing board
- Sizing in small bowl
- Paintbrush
- Awl
- Tweezers
- Iron
- Acetate
- Sharpie Ultra Fine Point permanent marker for very dark fabric

1. Place the fabric with the selected motif right side up on a lightbox. **FIGURE A**

2. Place the freezer paper, shiny side down, on top of the motif. Trace around the perimeter of the motif with pencil, creating a template pattern. Before you remove the freezer paper, turn off the lightbox and make sure you've traced the complete outline.

3. Pre-shrink the freezer paper. Layer the freezer paper with the traced template on top of a blank piece of freezer paper, shiny sides down, and fuse them together with a hot, dry iron.

4. Cut out the template, preserving the freezer paper window. **FIGURE B**

5. On the pressing board, place the template window precisely so that it frames the motif exactly. When satisfied with the window placement, heat press the window on the fabric with a hot, dry iron. **FIGURE C**

6. Insert the template inside the window. Heat press. Peel off the window, leaving the template adhered to the fabric. **FIGURE D**

7. Cut out around the template, adding a ⅛" seam allowance beyond the template edges.

Simply Successful Appliqué

8. Peel the template off the front of the fabric. Place the fabric cutout facedown and center the template, shiny side up, on top. Fold the fabric over the template at three places to stabilize the position of the template and heat tack the edges. Continue to turn over the fabric edges around the template perimeter, using an awl where needed and sizing to make edges malleable and folds crisp. **FIGURE E**

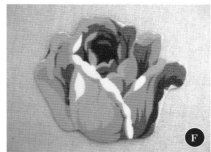

9. Examine the front side of the appliqué to make sure all edges are smooth. The shape is ready to appliqué. **FIGURE F**

 tip

Making Broderie Perse Templates for Dark Fabric

For darker fabric, the shape of a motif may be difficult to see clearly through the freezer paper, even when placed on a lightbox. Tracing a precise line around the perimeter is nearly impossible. In this case, place a sheet of clear acetate on top of the fabric motif and trace the shape with a fine-point permanent marker. Remove the fabric and place the acetate directly on the lightbox. Cover the acetate with freezer paper (shiny side down) and trace the image onto the freezer paper. Proceed to make the template, window, and Broderie Perse appliqué as described above.

Opportunities for Creative Interpretation

When I was planning to use Broderie Perse for the three main flowers in *Tweet Treats,* the rose as it appeared on the fabric was too large for the space allowed on the design. *No problem!* I studied the details on the rose and traced a simpler, smaller flower outline onto my freezer paper to get it to fit. The trimmed down version worked fine.

Blended-Edge Broderie Perse

In the above instructions, only one flower was used from a larger floral print. Another way to capitalize on the rich detail found in printed fabric is to use an entire design for Broderie Perse.

For this technique, the template outline is drawn to include some of the motif fabric background beyond the print edges, and a matching background color is chosen for the quilt to trick the eye into seeing the motif and quilt background as one. The motif is appliquéd, blending seamlessly into the background fabric. An advantage is that the detail of the fabric print remains, but the turned edges are merely broad curves surrounding the shapes, making it quick and easy to stitch them down. The effect is stunning!

This technique is seen in vintage chintz appliqué quilts, such as the quilt at right, made in the early 1800s.

Notice how the chintz print fabric is cut out beyond the motif and how the cream fabric blends into the cream background of the quilt.

Appliqué Lettering

There are many opportunities to add a word, phrase, monogram, and so on, to an appliqué piece for a special personalized touch. This tutorial features a cursive font style accomplished by combining appliqué letter elements with embroidered serifs and flourishes. NOTE: This tutorial focuses on making appliqué letters. For the complete album cover project instructions, see page CD140.

Memory album cover (page CD140) featuring appliqué lettering

Selecting a Lettering Font and Preparing a Master Pattern

1. Sketch a rough layout of what you want to write to see how you'd like the words arranged on your project. This will also give you a rough estimate of the space you need to allocate for the letters. Draw the area or field for the lettering full-size on graph paper.

2. Select a font that appeals to you (use your computer or another source). Enlarge the text to fit the design field—experiment as needed to get the correct size. If needed, cut apart the letters to place them as designed. Use clear tape to hold them in place on a piece of paper. Redraw any connecting lines or serifs. **FIGURE A**

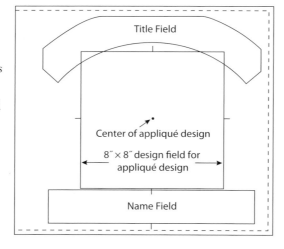

Title Field

Center of appliqué design

8″ × 8″ design field for appliqué design

Name Field

3. Make any desired changes to the letters (such as widening or changing a shape) by drawing over the basic letter strokes. Number each piece, including letters that will be made using 2 pieces, such as the *q.* **FIGURE B**

4. Audition the entire layout. When you're happy with the layout and any changes, make a photocopy that will become the master pattern from which you will make the templates and the overlay. **FIGURE C**

Making Letter Templates

1. Prepare a master copy of letters to be made into appliqués, a photocopy of the master (for a working copy), and an inkjet photocopy or traced copy of the master printed on stiff interfacing / Patch Back sheet or the equivalent stiff interfacing (page 8). If you are tracing, use a lightbox and a mechanical pencil.

 tip
Tips for Printing on Patch Back/Stiff Interfacing Sheets

- *Use the lightest copy setting on your copier/printer.*
- *Before working with your actual fabric, make a test sample of a printed template. Some copier inks bleed when glued or washed. Try heat setting with a hot iron.*

2. Cut out a letter segment from stiff interfacing / Patch Back. This is the foundation template. **FIGURE D**

3. Place the template (printed side facing up) on plain paper. Use a gluestick to apply an even layer of glue.

4. Place the appliqué fabric wrong side up on a hard work surface. Using tweezers, place the template glue side down on the fabric. Press with your fingertips to secure. Allow the glue to set a few minutes.

5. Cut out the fabric shape, adding a scant ⅛″ turn allowance to all edges. **FIGURE E**

6. Place the fabric cutout wrong side up on a piece of paper. Apply an even layer of glue to the template and fabric edges. **FIGURE F**

7. Hold down the shape with an awl while turning over the edges with a cuticle stick (or vice versa, whichever works best for you). The turning steps are the same as preturning edges when making any fabric appliqué (pages 27–43) but without using freezer paper, sizing, and iron.

8. After the first side edge is turned, turn the second edge. Do not cut off the flags at the points. **FIGURE G**

9. Reapply glue to the points. Turn over the flags onto the tip ends, tucking in all the excess fabric and stray threads inside the foundation edges. **FIGURE H**

10. With tweezers, flip the prepared appliqué piece to the right side, placing it on top of the master pattern copy to keep track of it. Repeat Steps 1–9 for all letter segments, a word at a time. **FIGURE I**

 tip *Preparing letter appliqués one word at a time is a practical way to stay organized. As each foundation template is glued face down on the fabric, label it with a pencil.*

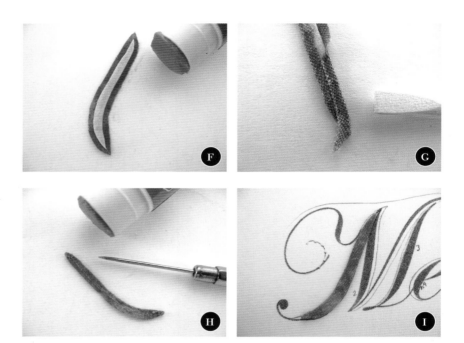

Stitching Appliqué Letters to the Background Fabric

1. Prepare an overlay for the lettering as you would for any appliqué design, including registration marks so the overlay matches up with the background fabric for precise letter placement (pages 46–48).

2. Glue-baste (page 51) the appliqué letter segments to the background fabric, using the overlay.

3. Appliqué the letter segments to the background fabric. For hand appliqué: Use stab stitches because the fabric will be a bit stiff from the glue (the glue will wash out and feel soft afterward). For machine appliqué: Engage the needle-down option (or manually operate the hand wheel), pivoting often for refined stitch placement on tight curves.

 tip
Machine Appliqué
If the machine foot is not level during stitching (causing the feed dogs to not work properly because of the raised letters), try placing a height-compensating plate (see the machine owner's manual) to the right of the foot, close to the needle, as you navigate around the pieces.

4. Transfer letter flourishes and serif design lines to the background fabric. Embroider with stem stitches to complete the scripted words. **FIGURE J**

Basic Embroidery Stitches

Straight Stitch

Up at 1 and down at 2.

Completed straight stitch

Backstitch

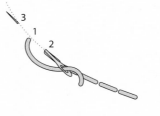

Satin Stitch

(Side-by-side straight stitches)

Stem Stitch

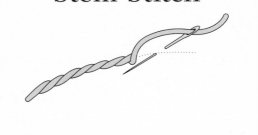

Padded Satin Stitch

(Vertical satin stitches covered by horizontal satin stitches)

Side-by-Side Stem Stitches

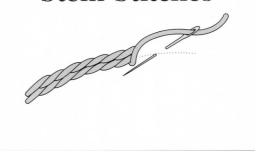

Lazy Daisy Stitch

A

B

C

Couching

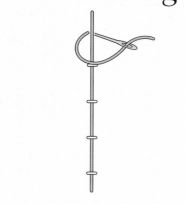

Chain Stitch

Bullion Knot

1
2

1
2

French Knot

1

2

3

Fly Stitch

1   2
3
4

Simply Successful Appliqué

About the Projects

Step-by-step project instructions and full-size template patterns can be found on the CD
All master patterns and templates are formatted for easy printouts on paper, freezer paper,
or transparencies for overlays, as needed.

The projects have been arranged to build skill upon skill. If you have worked through
the instructions in this book, you can certainly make any of the projects in any order.

The best example (and confidence builder) I can think of to share took place at the
end of a workshop. After everyone enjoyed "show and share" with a lot of *oooohs*
and *ahhhhs*, I asked if anyone might have a suggestion to help me improve upon the
instruction. One of the students declared she was really pleased with all she'd learned
and accomplished but thought that I should list the class for intermediate- and
advanced-level students because she thought it would have been hard for a beginner.
Before I could begin to respond, three students popped up to announce that they
were complete beginners (only I had known). Their work stood proud with the best.

How to Use the Projects

All the projects include a master pattern, individual template patterns, and step-
by-step assembly directions. The master patterns and templates are on the CD that
comes with this book. The master patterns are provided in a standard 12″ × 12″
design field, except the blocks in the *Just for Pretty* sampler, which are given in
4″ × 4″ design fields. All master patterns are full size, as are the template patterns.
Use the master pattern to make an overlay (pages 46–48). If you are planning to
reduce or enlarge the master pattern, the same print setting must be applied to all
pattern elements and templates. Adjust the number of strands and type of thread for
embroidery for reduced or enlarged blocks.

Assembly Guide

An assembly guide is included
with each project with a suggested
order for completing the project.
It may also direct you to specific
book pages for special techniques.

Most often, the assembly guide
will include options, so you can
choose from different versions of
how to make a flower or other
design element. Each option
has its own set of template
patterns, with labels prefaced by
a symbol such as a heart or star
to differentiate them from the
basic appliqué templates.

Finishing

For information on layering,
basting, quilting, and binding
a quilt, visit www.ctpub.com.
On the home page, scroll down
to Consumer Resources, select
Quiltmaking Basics, and choose
a tutorial topic.

This page includes examples of what is on the CD for each project.

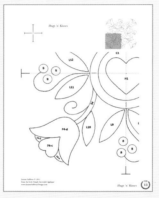 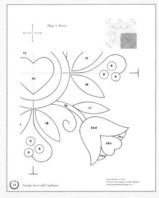

Hugs 'n' Kisses appliqué.
Designed and stitched by Jeanne Sullivan.
(For the full project, see pages CD7–CD17.)

Master pattern quadrants: Print and tape together to make master pattern and overlay.

- A photo of the finished project

- Quadrants of the master pattern to print on your home printer and tape together to make the master pattern and overlay

- 8½″ × 11″ pages of full-size templates to print on freezer paper using your home printer. No more tracing!

- 8½″ × 11″ pages of the assembly instructions to print on your home printer

tip *Don't have a home printer? No problem. Just bring your CD to the local print shop, and they'll be happy to copy what you need directly from the CD. Bring along some freezer paper plus some transparency sheets in case the copy shop doesn't stock them.*

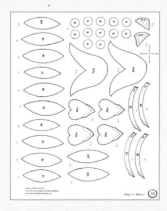 

Individual template pages to print on freezer paper

 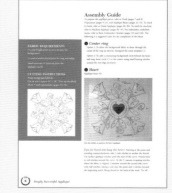

Assembly guide pages

Just for Pretty sampler, appliquéd and embroidered; then framed. Designed and stitched by Jeanne Sullivan. (For the full project, see pages CD18–CD35.)

Tweet Treats interpreted with dimensional floral elements, Broderie Perse, and reverse appliqué with embroidery embellishment. Designed and stitched by Jeanne Sullivan. (For the full project, see pages CD36–CD49.)

Sunflower Glory, created with plenty of easy dimensional elements, including an irresistible stuffed ladybug. Designed and made by Jeanne Sullivan. (For the full project, see pages CD50–CD64.)

A Basketful of Hope completed in vivid palette of classic Baltimore. Designed and made by Jeanne Sullivan. (For the full project, see pages CD65–CD88.)

Hope Sings, winner First Place Appliqué, Northcott Quest for a Cure Challenge 2006. Designed and made by Jeanne Sullivan using Northcott's Heaven on Earth fabric collection by Ro Gregg. (For the full project, see pages CD89–CD102.)

Hope Sweet Hope, winner First Place Appliqué, Northcott Quest for a Cure Challenge 2007. Second in the Hope series, designed and stitched by Jeanne Sullivan using Northcott's Heaven Can Wait fabric collection by Ro Gregg. (For the full project, see pages CD103–CD121.)

Springtime's Promise, designed and stitched by Jeanne Sullivan (For the full project, see pages CD122–CD139.)

Memories in Appliqué album cover. Designed and stitched by Jeanne Sullivan. (For the full project, see pages CD140–CD152.)

Resources

Suppliers

Support your local quilt shop!

Jeanne Sullivan Design
www.JeanneSullivanDesign.com
800-593-4181
Simply Successful Appliqué supplies, Patch Back, Shadow Block, tracing bridges, scissors, awls, notions, Ruche Mark ruching guides, chatelaines, and more

C&T Publishing
www.ctpub.com
C&T blog: www.ctpubblog.com
Stash Books blog: www.stashbooksblog.com
Pattern Spot: www.patternspot.com
800-284-1114

Northcott Silk Inc.
www.northcott.com; www.northcott.net
800-268-1466
Cotton fabrics that feel like silk; current and soon-to-be-released fabric collections; and shop locator

Maria's Picture Place
www.mariaspictureplace.com
410-263-8282
Custom framing experts (and perfectionists!) specializing in framed heirloom stitchery and appliqué

Marlene Chaffey—teacher, lecturer, designer
Email: m.chaffey47@gmail.com
Phone (calling from U.S.): 011-44-1647-61262
(calling from within UK): 0-1647-61262
Twiscombe Farm, Whitestone
Exeter, EX4 2HS, Devon, UK
Contact Marlene for her current Fancy Free workshop program and information.

Seminole Sampler
www.seminolesampler.com
866-407-2363
Well-stocked quilt shop with a most welcoming and knowledgeable staff

Organizations

Try to join a local guild or small bee, if you can, for the camaraderie as much as the inspiration and motivation. Guild newsletters and organization journals are a rich source for current trends, interesting and entertaining articles, show calendars, contest details, and more. Here are some favorites:

American Quilter's Society
www.AmericanQuilter.com

The American Quilt Study Group
www.americanquiltstudygroup.org

The Appliqué Society
www.theappliquesociety.org

Baltimore Appliqué Society
www.BaltimoreApplique.com

International Quilt Association
www.quilts.org

The National Quilting Association
www.nqaquilts.org

Books

Collins, Sally. *Mastering Precision Piecing.* Lafayette, California: C&T Publishing, 2006.

Dietrich, Mimi. *Mimi Dietrich's Baltimore Basics: Album Quilts from Start to Finish.* Woodinville, Washington: Martingale & Company, 2006.

Hargrave, Harriet. *Mastering Machine Appliqué.* Lafayette, California: C&T Publishing, 2001.

Mech, Dr. Susan Delaney. *Rx for Quilters.* Lafayette, California: C&T Publishing (eBook available), 2000.

Tools

Wolfrom, Joen. Ultimate 3-in-1 Color Tool. Lafayette, California: C&T Publishing, 2006.

About the Author

"My mother said I must have been vaccinated with a phonograph needle because I was always singing and talking her ear off. I think she was wrong.… It must have been a sewing needle!" —Jeanne

Fiber artist Jeanne Sullivan can't remember a time when she wasn't enjoying a creative love affair with needle, thread, and hook. For Jeanne, the seeds of passion were "sewn" when she was a very young child, stitching small cross-stitch motifs that her mother would draw for her on scraps of fabric. Growing up, she always had a project going—sewing her own clothes, embroidery, knitting, and crochet. Early in her teaching career, Jeanne became totally obsessed with making yo-yos—completing a 2,700-yo-yo quilt while sitting in stalled Long Island traffic on her way to work. Then a quilt exhibit ignited her interest, and she set about creating a design for a pillow, puzzling out a way to appliqué on her own without the benefit of books or instruction. The die was cast: That little project spurred an interest in appliqué that knows no bounds.

Raising a family along with the demands of serving as an elementary school principal left little time for playful meandering; however, now retired, Jeanne spends nearly every waking hour happily immersed in mountains of fabric, leaving a thread trail wherever she goes. While her first love remains appliqué, Jeanne also enjoys traditional rug hooking, spinning, and weaving.

Recognized for her beautiful appliqué designs and outstanding needle skills, Jeanne has been the recipient of Best of Show and Heirloom Quilter awards and has secured top honors for her appliqué in the international Northcott Quest for a Cure Challenge for three consecutive years. Her unique blend of traditional and dimensional appliqué along with Broderie Perse and embroidery embellishment gives her work distinctive appeal. Jeanne delights in teaching hand and machine appliqué using her simplified, success-oriented methods. She hopes that the fine art of appliqué will take up its proper place as an easy and enjoyable needleart technique. Jeanne's explicit instruction and straightforward techniques make this a realistic goal for anyone willing to give it a try.

Jeanne now calls Annapolis, Maryland, home. Visit the author's website, www.JeanneSullivanDesign.com, or call 800-593-4181.

Great Titles and Products

from C&T PUBLISHING

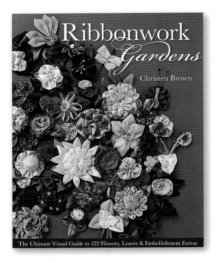

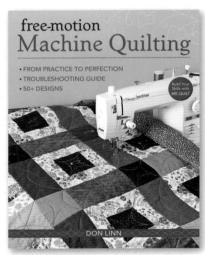

Available at your local retailer or **www.ctpub.com** *or* **800-284-1114**

For a list of other fine books from C&T Publishing, visit our website to view our catalog online.

C&T PUBLISHING, INC.
P.O. Box 1456
Lafayette, CA 94549 | Email: ctinfo@ctpub.com
800-284-1114 | Website: www.ctpub.com

C&T Publishing's professional photography services are now available to the public. Visit us at www.ctmediaservices.com.

Tips and Techniques *can be found at www.ctpub.com > Consumer*

For quilting supplies:

COTTON PATCH
1025 Brown Ave.
Lafayette, CA 94549
Store: 925-284-1177 | Email: CottonPa@aol.com
Mail order: 925-283-7883 | Website: www.quiltusa.com

Note: Fabrics shown may not be currently available, as fabric manufacturers keep most fabrics in print for only a short time.